MR FABULOUS:
Memoirs of the Hollywood Life

By Steven Capozzola

MR FABULOUS: Memoirs of the Hollywood Life

By Steven Capozzola

Copyright 1998, 2002, 2018

This is a work of fiction. Any resemblance between the characters contained within, and actual persons, living or dead, is entirely coincidental. No celebrities were harmed during the production of this book.

Many of these stories first appeared in The San Francisco Herald. Special thanks to Herald editor Gene Mahoney.

Cover illustration by Dan Wlffler.

As We Go Up We Go Down

There was one time when I got stuck in an elevator with Michael Bolton and Richard Nixon. It was during the annual Breast Cancer Benefit at the L.A. Hyatt. I was there escorting Sheena Easton. My agent had arranged for Sheena to sing a medley during the night's show; he thought it would be nice if Sheena and I were photographed together.

We had arrived at the benefit at 8 pm. During Bea Arthur's keynote speech, I gave Sheena a quick kiss on the cheek and drifted downstairs to the Fairmont Room. I ordered a scotch-on-the-rocks and then strolled through the south wing. I sipped my drink and studied some of the photographs on the Wall of Fame. Then I hopped into an elevator to return to the ballroom. When I stepped into the elevator, I noticed an older man, dressed in a charcoal-gray suit, staring at the elevator wall. He was muttering to himself. Next to him stood a younger man in a navy blue suit. The door closed and the elevator started climbing.

At the next floor, Michael Bolton stepped into the elevator. I recognized his distinctive, shoulder-length blonde hair immediately. I jumped toward him, almost spilling my drink.

"Michael, baby—how cool to run into you. How'ya doing, man?"

Michael looked down at the floor. "Hey..."

I patted him on the shoulder. "Mike, you are just awesome. Just awesome. I love your stuff."

He nodded and looked at the floor. "Uhh, thanks."

I had a huge smile on my face. "I have to tell you, your song, 'When A Man's Got A Good Woman'—that song just slays me. It just kills me. I love it. Did you write that?"

Michael kept staring at the floor of the elevator. He didn't answer. I poked him in the arm. "Hey, you wrote that, right?"

He looked up at me quickly, then looked away. He shook his head and said softly, "No, I didn't write it."

I nodded. "Well, it's great. It just tears me up inside. 'When A Man Needs A Good Woman.' Yeah, I can really dig where you're coming from."

"It's called 'When A Man Loves A Woman.'"

"Oh, right."

I paused. "You know, Mike, there was this period of time not too long ago when I wasn't working. And that song came out and I heard it on the radio, and it was just—your voice was so right on. I mean, you have more soul than anybody, man. You're really great. Has anybody ever told you how much soul you have? I mean, you're fantastic."

Michael was looking at the floor. "Thanks."

I nodded. "Yeah."

Suddenly the lights in the elevator blinked off for a moment. And then they blinked on again. And then the elevator suddenly lurched to a stop. I stumbled sideways, bumping into the old man in the charcoal suit. Some of my drink splashed on the sleeve of my sport jacket.

"Excuse me—"

"Hey—" The guy in the navy blue suit pushed me away from the old man. "Step back, please."

"Huh?" I stepped away from the old man. The guy in the navy suit steadied the old man. "Mr. President, are you okay, sir?"

The old man raised his head. It was Richard Nixon. I was startled. Nixon nodded his head. "Just fine, son."

The young guy glanced up at the ceiling of the elevator. "We seem to have stopped, sir. Possibly the elevator's malfunctioned. I'll radio for help."

Nixon nodded. "All right."

The young guy pulled a walkie-talkie out of his suit jacket. "Lone Wolf to Silver Bird, Lone Wolf to Silver Bird, do you copy, over?"

I poked Michael Bolton. "Hot damn, it's Richard Nixon. Can you believe it?"

The young guy put an arm in front of me. "Take it easy. Step back, please."

I smiled. "No problem here." I shook my head. "But wow, Richard Nixon—what are you doing here?"

The young guy pointed at me. "Look, sir, please just step back. You're interfering with official business."

"Hey, man, I'm cool."

He clicked the radio again. "Lone Wolf to Silver Bird, do you copy, over?..."

The radio crackled with static. After a moment a voice answered faintly, "Roger, Lone Wolf."

The young guy nodded to himself and spoke into the radio. "Uhh, Jim... Mother Goose needs help in the south elevator."

The radio voice crackled, "That's a roger, Lone Wolf."

I turned to Michael Bolton. He was looking at Richard Nixon. "Pretty cool, huh?"

"Sure."

I turned to Nixon. He was standing quietly in a corner of the elevator. "So, Mr. President... how are you? How's retirement treating you?"

Nixon nodded. "Pretty good—as long as this elevator gets going."

I laughed. "Right, right..." I turned and indicated Michael Bolton. "Mr. President, do you know Michael Bolton?"

"No, I don't."

"He's great. A famous singer. He's got a couple of gold albums."

Michael flashed a beaming smile at Nixon. "Platinum albums, actually."

I nodded. "Yeah, he's an amazing singer."

Nixon reached to shake Michael Bolton's hand. The secret service guy paused. He glanced from Nixon to Michael Bolton to Nixon. "Uh, Mr. President?..."

Nixon turned to him. "It's okay, son." He reached out and shook Michael Bolton's hand.

Michael Bolton grinned. "It's a pleasure."

I turned to Nixon. "So what are you doing here?"

"Pat insisted we do the benefit this year."

"Well...what do you think?"

Nixon frowned. "A huge fuss. All these jackasses making speeches. I can't get a drink to save my life."

I glanced at my half-finished scotch-on-the-rocks. "Hey, I'm drinking scotch if you want some."

I held out my glass to Nixon. He started to reach for it. Suddenly, the secret service guy, who'd been talking on his walkie-talkie, reached out and grabbed my drink. He turned to Nixon. "Mr. President, I really must insist…"

Nixon exploded. "God-damnit, son—gimme that scotch."

The secret service guy handed over the glass. Nixon slugged it down. Then he exhaled. "Whooh—good stuff. Wish I had another."

I smiled. "I hear that. Believe me, if we weren't stuck in this elevator, I think I'd turn right around and head back to the bar."

Nixon nodded. "You're my kind of man."

Michael Bolton gestured at Nixon. "I love a good Sauvignon Blanc myself."

Nixon squinted at Michael Bolton. "What?"

Michael smiled a beaming smile. "I always love a good white wine. Nothing too tart. But anything French'll work for me. What about you?"

Nixon shook his head. He turned to me. "What's wrong with this guy?"

I chuckled. "I hear you."

Nixon elbowed me. "I mean, I thought he had a sissy boy haircut. But what's all this wine crap?"

I nodded my head solemnly. "I know it."

The secret service guy clicked off his walkie-talkie. "Good news, gentleman. The elevator should come back any sec—"

Just at that moment the elevator lurched upward again. I stumbled sideways, but Nixon grabbed my arm to steady me. I looked up at him. "Thanks."

"No problem."

The secret service guy gestured with his walkie-talkie. "They were just switching the power downstairs or something."

We all nodded. "Uh-huh."

Nixon turned to me. "Listen, I'm sure this whole show's gonna be a piss-poor bore. But why don't you join me at my table? We'll knock back a couple more glasses."

"Thanks, man. That'd be swell—that is, just as long as there's room for my lady friend..."

Nixon pointed at Michael Bolton. "You mean blondie, there?"

I laughed. "Right, right." I chuckled. "No, seriously, I'm here with a lovely redhead. She's a singer. Her name's Sheena Easton."

Nixon nodded. "Oh, right. Terrific girl. Did the James Bond song."

"She's the one."

"Great. She and Pat will get along fabulously."

"All right."

We rode the elevator up to the ballroom.

The Winner and Still Champ

My agent had scheduled me for a lunch meeting at Ed Silver Productions to discuss Sylvester Stallone's upcoming project, 'Arsenal: The Return.' Ed himself would be there. He wanted to speak with me, man-to-man, to size me up for the job.

On the way to Ed's office, I stopped at the Torino Deli and grabbed a bagel-and-lox to go. Sebastian took my order. He wrapped up my bagel with a pickle and added my usual Prince Iced Tea. I paid at the cash register and walked out.

I started walking along Hollywood Boulevard. Suddenly I spotted Julia Roberts and her curly auburn hair walking a few yards in front of me. Julia had just stepped out of Nata's Big Salads and was striding along the sidewalk carrying a brown lunchbag. I hurried off toward her.

Near Vine Street, I drew up next to her. As I did so, I leaned toward her and said, "UH-OH...LOOK OUT...my lunch is RAPIDLY catching up with yours, and...look out...it's taking the lead now...and...WHOOSH...it's leaving yours in the dust..." I turned to her and smiled, giving her my good-as-candy smile. Then I pivoted and started to race ahead of her.

But Julia whirled at me. "JESUS. WHAT THE HELL?"

I slowed down and looked back at her. "What's the matter?"

"YOU ASSHOLE. YOU SCARED THE HELL OUT OF ME."

"Baby, I'm not that scary looking. Some people think I'm kinda handsome."

Julia pointed a finger at me. Her hand was shaking. "I thought you were a terrorist or something. DON'T YOU KNOW WHAT'S GOING ON IN THE WORLD? What the hell's wrong with you?"

"Oh come on. I was racing your lunchbag."

Julia squinted at me. "WHAT?"

"I was racing your lunchbag. And mine was clearly winning. Freddie and I were passing you like a Volkswagen stalled on the Santa Ana."

Julia put her hand to her forehead. "God, you're just some nut."

"No I'm not. I used to race Tom Hanks on Los Feliz all the time. He'd have a chicken salad on wheat bread from Paco's. I'd have a burrito from Si Senor. A burrito's much more aerodynamic. I'd leave him sucking wind like a gullyfish."

Julia started walking away from me. Her shoes made quick scuffing sounds against the sidewalk. I called after her. "Uh-oh, Julia's making a late surge..."

I balanced my lunch and started racing after her. I was amazed. Julia was moving like Ben Affleck at The Swizzle Stick. I shouted after her, "Baby, no one's taken me in almost seven years...YOU CAN RUN, BUT YOU CAN'T HIDE..." I began to really move. "I'm carrying a 32-ounce iced tea, and I'm STILL gonna catch you...No one's gonna take me on my HOME TURF."

Soon I was sweating. But I was gaining ground. I watched Julia switch her lunchbag from one hand to the other. I recognized that move. She was beginning to falter. It was only a matter of time.

I stepped through the Del Rey intersection and, by the next corner, had drawn up parallel to her. I nodded quickly. "Thanks for playing." Then I breezed past her.

I hit the sidewalk and accelerated, leaving her trailing in my wake.

When You Gotta Eat, You Gotta Eat

Whoopi called me at 4 pm on a Tuesday afternoon. She said that she needed a date for Sally Struthers' Annual Hungerthon Dinner that night. Would I go with her? She promised that there'd be a full dinner and lots of wine. I said, "I'll be there, baby."

I was supposed to meet her at 7 pm at The Regency Hotel. That left time for me to cram in a full workout at Biceptual, the new gym that Richard Gere had opened with Tom Cruise. I drove over to the gym and spent an hour on the bike. Then I lifted weights for about 30 minutes. By the time I finished my last set of free weights, I was feeling incredibly weak. I was ravenous with hunger and my arms felt like lead. As I showered, my legs began to stiffen from the exercise bike. I dressed as quickly as I could, then squeezed into my Hyundai and raced over to The Regency.

I was running late by the time I arrived at the hotel. I ran inside and found Whoopi waiting for me at the bar. She was talking to Brad Pitt and Ashton Kutcher. They were debating whether or not Winona Ryder looked exactly like the kid in 'Lord of the Rings.' Whoopi jumped up as I greeted her. She gave me a big kiss on the cheek, then quickly introduced me to Brad and Ashton.

"Hey guys."

"Hey."

"Hi."

Whoopi handed me a glass of red wine. We said a hurried goodbye to Brad and Ashton, then walked quickly to the ballroom.

As we stepped into the hall, Whoopi nudged my shoulder. "You look all buff."

"Yeah, I just got through working out. But listen, I'm starving. When do we eat?"

"Soon. We just have to wait for Sally to make a speech. Then they'll serve dinner."

"All right. I hope she makes it quick, though. I'm starting to get lightheaded."

Whoopi poked my arm. "God. You're always such a baby."

We walked to our table and took our seats. I noticed Drew Barrymoore and David Lane sitting next to us. They had their chairs turned toward the podium. We sat down.

Just at that moment, the whole room stood up and began applauding as Sally Struthers stepped up to the podium. There was a long round of clapping. Then everyone sat down.

Sally looked out at the audience and paused. The room fell absolutely quiet. Someone coughed at a nearby table.

Sally looked down at her speech for a moment. She cleared her throat. "Eight million," she said. She paused for a moment as her voice echoed through the large hall. She repeated herself: "Eight million." Then she looked out at the audience and said, "Eight million children will die of hunger this year."

I turned to Whoopi and whispered, "Eight million and one if I don't eat something soon."

Whoopi put a finger to her lips. "Shhh..."

Sally began to launch into her speech. It was something about hunger in Africa and Asia and a lack of running water. I took a sip of my wine. It went immediately to my head. I felt a sudden tightening in the front of my skull. I knew that I needed water.

There was a glass of water set in front of me on the table. I grabbed the glass and drank the whole thing down. Then I looked around for a waiter to pour a refill. I couldn't spot one. But I noticed a large metal waiter's tray resting on a fold-up stand next to our table. It was holding a half-empty pitcher of water. I leaned over and grabbed the pitcher. I poured myself another glass of water.

Sally talked on. She was mentioning something about the United Nations. I began to feel light-headed. My blood sugar was getting too low. My head and neck felt uncomfortably warm. I turned to Whoopi.

"Hey...I gotta eat something...I'm getting lightheaded."

Whoopi waved me away with her hand. I leaned toward her and whispered, "But I'm really feeling faint."

Whoopi whispered back. "Why didn't you eat before you got here?"

"I didn't have time. I had to get to the gym. And you said they'd be serving dinner."

"Why didn't you eat a power bar or something?"

"I forgot to."

"Well then, that's your problem."

Whoopi sat back in her chair. I took a deep breath. I leaned back in my chair and slowly exhaled. I began to massage my forehead.

Sally's speech continued. She passed the 10-minute mark. Little parts of her speech filtered in and out of my consciousness: "World Health Organization...50,000 rations per day...if we sit idly by...vaccination teams...hookworm and ringworm...agriculture department...wheat and grain surplus..."

After a few more minutes I turned to Whoopi. "I think I'm digesting my spleen right now."

"Oh hush up."

"But I feel faint."

"She'll be done soon."

"Yeah, but when?"

"I don't know."

I sat back in my chair and began to glance around the room. I spotted Lindsay Wagner and Andy Garcia sitting at a nearby table; Lindsay was yawning. I turned back to Whoopi. "I'll bet everybody's just waiting to eat."

Whoopi looked at me. "Yeah, but they're behaving like adults."

"But I'm really feeling faint...I gotta do something..."

"Shhh."

I looked around the room. At various tables, I could see people fidgeting and yawning. I noticed Lee Majors sitting at a side table. He was holding his head in his hands. He looked exhausted.

Sally's voice droned on: "a concerted effort...political involvement...for just pennies a day..."

A wave of nausea rippled through me. I felt close to fainting. I looked around at another table, then noticed the waiter's stand parked next to our table. It held a large silver tray almost two feet in diameter.

With the last of my strength, I lifted myself out of my chair and stepped over to the tray. I could feel my heart pounding mightily in my chest. All the blood seemed to drain out of my head. I began to see gray.

I picked up the tray with my left hand. My arm trembled from workout fatigue. I held the tray up in the air like a mirror. Then, with a quick punch of my right fist, I gonged the tray as loudly as I could. It sent an enormous metal boom reverberating through the hall.

Instantly the whole room jumped. Everyone turned to look.

People stared at me. I nodded at them and quickly replaced the tray on its stand. Then I sat down next to Whoopi; she was covering her face with her hands.

At the podium, Sally stumbled for something to say. For a moment she looked down at her speech. But then she interrupted herself. "I think...uhhh...we'll, uhh...we'll finish here and...just...thank you..."

The audience stood up and began to applaud. I turned to Whoopi. "See, now we'll get to eat."

I sat back in my chair and waited for dinner to be served.

All Aboard

I'm not sure when it was, or for what movie, but my agent sent me to New York for a movie audition. I flew into New York and took a cab to midtown Manhattan. I found myself hurrying down the main escalator of Grand Central Station, in a rush to catch a train to my audition. I had probably a minute-and-a-half to make a train on the lower level. I was sort of pushing my way down the escalator, ducking past people, muttering, "Excuse me, excuse me." Near the bottom of the escalator, I half-stumbled into a short, dark-haired woman.

"Pardon me," I said.

The woman poked me in the shoulder. "Why don't you watch where you going? You knock me over, why not?"

I continued down the escalator. I half-turned to the woman. "Sorry, baby—I gotta make a train." I continued jostling down the escalator. "Excuse me, excuse me..."

Behind me, the dark-haired woman shouted, "'BABY'—you don't call me 'baby.'"

I ignored her and jumped down the last few steps of the escalator. I landed on the tan marble floor of Grand Central's main hall. I began hurrying toward the north stairwell. I had less than a minute to get to the lower level and catch my train.

I hadn't gone more than 10 steps when someone crashed into me. I fell forward, landing flat on my hands and knees. My Bitterman trenchcoat—which I'd been carrying over my right arm—draped itself across the floor.

A woman's voice shouted behind me, "That's for calling me 'baby.'"

I stood up and turned around. It was the dark-haired woman from the escalator. She was wearing large wraparound sunglasses and a black leather jacket. Her face looked familiar. She touched her bun of hair to steady it. I suddenly realized that I was looking at Yoko Ono.

I hurriedly picked up my trenchcoat. "My God, Yoko, honey—I had no idea it was you."

Yoko glared at me. "You a very bad person."

I folded my trenchcoat. "Oh, baby—don't say that. You gotta forgive me. See, I just gotta make this train." I turned and pointed at the stairwell to the lower level. "See, I gotta go. All right, honey?... Everything's cool, right? Okay, bye..."

Yoko stomped her foot. "No, no. You say sorry, right now."

I was frantic to make my train. "No, Yoko—I love you, baby, you know that."

"Say sorry."

I had to think quickly. "My God," I shouted. "What's that?" I pointed to something behind Yoko. She turned to look, putting up a hand to steady her hair. Instantly I sprinted off to the stairwell.

I jumped down the first part of the stairs. Behind me Yoko began shouting, "Creep, creep..."

I jumped the final steps to the lower level. I could hear the clip-clop of Yoko's feet echoing behind me in the stairwell. She was chasing after me. I ran down the hall to my train's gate. I ducked through the gate and sprinted down the ramp leading to the platform.

Yoko saw me run through the gate. She began shrieking something unintelligible, "Eeeeeeeeeeehhh..."

I spotted my train waiting along the platform. At that moment, a bell sounded. Just as I reached the first car of the train, the door slid shut in front of me.

I panted frantically. I glanced back at Yoko and began pounding on the door of the train.

"Please, somebody. For God's sake—open the door..."

I pounded on the door again. A Metro-North conductor walked by; he ignored me.

I glanced back again at Yoko. She was bounding down the ramp. Her bun of hair was flopping loosely around her ears. I pushed off the door of the train and began sprinting down the platform.

I ran past the next car, and then past the dining car, trying to put some distance between me and Yoko. I glanced back and saw her lurching clumsily along, half-trying to steady her hair. Stray black hairs had fallen across her sunglasses.

The bell of the train rang again. I ran to the next car and began pounding on the door. "Please somebody—anybody. Help me. God—"

A conductor appeared in front of the door. He was holding a clipboard. He yelled through the window, "You got a ticket?"

"Yes, yes," I shouted, still pounding on the glass. "I have a ticket."

"Let me see it."

I reached into my pocket to pull out my round-trip voucher. I glanced back at Yoko. She had pulled a hairpin out of her hair. She was charging toward me, holding the hairpin like a knife in her hand. All her hair had flopped down crazily around her face. She saw me glance at her and began to shout, "AIGHHH..."

I dug out my voucher and held it up for the conductor. "Please, hurry. She's gonna kill me..."

The conductor glanced at my ticket. Then he reached up and pushed the door release button. A bell rang and the door slid open. I fell inside, panting and wheezing.

"Oh, thank Christ," I gasped. "Thank you, Lord."

The conductor released the button and the door slid shut. Just at that moment, Yoko leaped for the door. I looked up in time to see her face bounce off the window. She fell back onto the platform.

The Metro-North conductor didn't seem to notice Yoko caroming off the door. He reached down and helped me to my feet. "Let me have your ticket."

I handed him my round-trip voucher. The train began to rumble down the track.

The Bat Cave

It was the Barry White CD that put Candace Bergen in the mood. We were at my place, fooling around on my green leather couch. I'd switched on the ceiling fan disco light. As I kissed Candace, flashes of silver light darted around the room. I unbuttoned her shirt, then stood up and walked over to the kitchen. I opened the fridge and cracked open a Budweiser. I slugged some down. "Ahh..."

I could hear Candace rolling around on the couch. Her pants were making rubbing noises against the leather. I stuck my head out of the kitchen. "Don't start without me."

I walked back out to the living room. Candace's hair was draped over the armrest of the couch. I sat down next to her and put my hand on her leg. "You want a sip of my beer?"

"Sure."

She took a sip and handed it back to me. I took another sip and rubbed her leg. She looked up at me and squinted. "You know, I just figured out why you look so familiar."

"Yeah? Why's that?"

"Weren't you in that commercial? The one with the woman scrubbing the bathtub?"

"Yeah. That was me."

"And there's these guys in football uniforms, and they suddenly appear in the bathtub. They're the cleaning team."

"Yeah, that was me, baby."

Candace started laughing. "You were one of the football players."

"Yup."

She tried to sit up. "Which one were you?"

"I had the blue uniform on. No helmet. I was the quarterback."

"Right." She nodded her head. "But you looked so much thinner."

"It was a couple of years ago."

Candace laughed. I put my arm around her and helped her to sit up. I looked at her. "You know, I'm not really interested in commercials. They're not the right vehicle for me."

"What's the right vehicle for you?"

"I need a serious project, like a drama."

"Oh."

I stood up. "Come on. I'll get you a beer."

Candace lifted herself up from the couch. I steered her toward the kitchen. Barry White's voice was purring from the stereo speakers.

Candace leaned against my shoulder. "It's so dark in here."

"No problem." I walked over to the coffee table and switched on my Suzanne Somers Commemorative lava lamp. Red light oozed through the room.

"Does this help?"

"Sort of."

Candace stepped away from me and looked at some of the photos on the wall near the kitchen. "You have so many pictures of yourself."

"Yeah, maybe..."

I finished my beer and grabbed two fresh Buds from the fridge. I handed one to Candace. We cracked our beers and took a few gulps. Candace looked around my condo.

"God, this place is like the inside of a spaceship. I feel like I'm in a UFO."

I took a sip of beer. Candace swayed for a moment. She walked out to the living room and stood over my black vinyl massage chair. "What's this?"

I walked up behind her and put my arms around her. "That's my Cool Papa massage chair. Only 3,000 of them were hand-built by Cool Papa in his lifetime."

"Oh."

I rubbed Candace's stomach.

"And what's that?" She pointed to my Bob Ketler smoke machine.

"Oh, that? That's my smoke machine."

"What's it for?"

"It makes smoke." I walked over and switched it on. After a few seconds, a thin mist of smoke began to waft along the floor. "Sometimes I like to set a mood."

"Oh."

"Come on." I took Candace's hand. "I'll show you the bedroom."

I walked her down the hall. Her bare feet stumbled in my purple shag carpeting. She looked down at her feet. "Wow, look at that. The carpet changes color as you walk on it."

"Yeah. It's static-charged."

I pushed open the wood-paneled door to my bedroom. I reached in and switched on the fluorescent track light along the left ceiling mirror. "Here we are."

Candace stepped into the bedroom. I followed her. She paused for a moment and looked down. "The floor feels weird."

"Oh yeah, it's sheet rubber. Easier to clean."

"Oh."

She turned to look at the full-length poster of me next to my lucite dresser. She pointed at the poster. "You look a lot younger in that."

"Yeah, maybe. I was a lifeguard back then." I finished my beer. "You want another beer?"

Candace lifted her beer. "No, I have this."

"All right."

I walked over to the mini-bar next to my night table. I reached into the cooler and grabbed a cold wet can of Budweiser. It was the last one. I cracked it open and took a sip.

Candace looked around the room. "I don't see a bed."

I jumped up. "Oh, right." I ran over to the closet doors and slid them open. I pressed the electric switch that automatically lowered my vinyl Murphy bed. The motor in the wall made a slow groaning noise as the bed lowered to the floor.

I pointed to the bed. "Here you go."

Candace tried to sit down. She lost her balance and fell off.

I reached to help her stand up. "Sorry. I forgot to tell you, it's a water bed."

"A water bed?"

"Yeah. Cool Papa built it about a year before he died. It's the only vinyl, fold-up water bed in Burbank."

Candace sat down slowly on the bed. She adjusted herself to the rhythm of the water. "Wow."

I sat down next to her. I took a sip of my beer. "How'ya feeling?"

"A little tired."

"Well, you're in the right place."

I pressed a button on my night table to lower down a pair of velcro-leather handcuffs. "Put these on. I'll give you a massage."

Candace looked at the handcuffs for a moment. "What are these?"

"Handcuffs, baby. You know, to hold you in place."

"Are you serious?"

"Sure."

She looked at me for a moment. "Why don't YOU put them on?"

"Really?"

"Yeah. You put them on. I'll give you a massage."

"You think so?"

"Sure. I'll tie you up."

I nodded. "Let me finish my beer." I took a few more swallows and gulped down the rest of my beer. I crushed the can and tossed it through the mini-basketball hoop attached to my bathroom door.

I smiled. "You want me to take off my shirt?"

She nodded. "Yeah. Why don't you do that?"

I unzipped my shirt. For a moment the zipper caught on one of my chest hairs. I yanked hard and pulled the zipper all the way down. I threw the shirt on the floor.

Candace reached across the bed and began wrapping the leather straps around my wrists. She tightened them and closed the velcro flaps. She looked at me. "You could get out of these if you had to, right?"

I nodded. "Sure thing. Probably take me two minutes. Maybe less."

"Good."

Candace began walking out of the bedroom.

I called after her. "Hey, can you get me one, too?"

I waited for Candace to bring me back a beer. She seemed to be taking a while.

"Candy?"

I tried to swing my head around toward the living room. The handcuffs were too tight. "Candy?..."

Just then I heard the front door open and close.

Kathie Lee

Some time after I'd returned from an audition in New York, I learned that Kathie Lee Gifford would be appearing at Mutrie's Rare Books to sign copies of her new book, 'Through the Laughter and the Tears.' I'd always been a big fan, even after all that had happened between us. So I made sure to get to the bookstore early.

I drifted around the back of the store and glanced through Sam Donaldson's autobiography, 'Candy and Wine.' A woman with red hair, late-thirties, was browsing the aisle next to me. She sort of half-turned once or twice, vaguely nodding at me. Gradually, she caught my eye, then finally smiled and said, "Hello."

I smiled back.

She turned to face me. "I'm Sherrie."

"I'm Gideon."

We shook hands.

Just at that moment, Kathie Lee breezed by. She noticed me and stopped in her tracks. She spun around on her high heels.

"Steve—my God, how are you?"

We hugged. Her perfume smelled amazing—a sort of coconut and pineapple mixture. I gave her a kiss on the cheek.

"Mm-hmm, Kath—you're like a great, big, yummy pina colada." I hugged her again. "I just wanna sit by the pool and sip you like a—"

Kathie Lee pinched my cheeks playfully. "God, you never change."

The woman with red hair, who'd just introduced herself as Sherrie, glared at me. "You said your name was Gideon."

I turned to her quickly. "Sometimes it is." I turned back to Kathie Lee. "Kath, you gotta tell me—whatever happened to that pilot? I was sure that—"

Sherrie interrupted. "That wasn't very nice. Why'd you lie about your name?"

Kathie Lee glanced at the redhead. Then she frowned at me. "Who's the tart?"

I shook my head. "I dunno. She was sort of hitting on me."

Sherrie stomped her foot. "I wasn't hitting on you."

"Yes you were."

"No I wasn't."

Kathie Lee waved her hands in the air. "I gotta get some coffee. This is too tedious for me."

"All right."

Kathie Lee walked off. I turned to Sherrie. "Thanks a lot."

Sherrie glared at me. She had nice blue eyes. I looked down to check her ankles, but she was wearing long dress pants. I raised my head again. Sherrie was still glaring. "What'd I do?"

"You made me look bad in front of Kathie Lee Gifford."

"That wasn't Kathie Lee Gifford?"

"Yeah it was."

"No it wasn't."

"Yes it was. She's signing her book here today. Last week, Lee Majors was here. They try to do a different celebrity each week."

"Really?"

"Yeah."

She shook her head. "I can't believe that was Kathie Lee Gifford. I mean, did you see how much make-up she had on. She looks like a whore. I'd never wear that much blush."

"I can't really talk about it. We used to date. So, you know—I can't..."

"You used to date Kathie Lee Gifford?"

"Sure. I love older women."

"Come on?"

I coughed. "Jeez, you don't believe anything I tell you."

"Well, it's kinda hard to believe that you dated Kathie Lee Gifford."

"Why?"

"Well, you're kinda chubby. But you are cute, in a sort of overgrown-kid kind of way."

"Hmm, it's funny you should say that."

"Why?"

"Because Barbra Streisand said the same thing about me. I think she did—or maybe I'm just remembering it wrong."

"Barbra Streisand?"

"Yeah."

She shook her head. "You talk a really good game."

I smiled. "I'm trying."

She paused for a moment. "Here." She took a pen and pad out of her purse. "This is my home number. But don't call after 5 or 5:30—my husband'll be home." She scribbled a number and handed it to me.

"Cool."

"Call me."

I shook her hand. "All right."

I watched her walk toward the front of the store. Just then, someone tapped me on the shoulder. I spun around. It was Kathie Lee. She was sipping a styrofoam cup of coffee. She frowned. "Where'd that bitch go?"

I ducked my head instinctively. "Shhh."

"Oh, come on. What do you care about her?"

"She liked me."

"She liked you?"

"Yeah."

"God, every girl always wants you. You're always saying, 'Oh, she wanted me.'" She took a sip of coffee. She swallowed and shook her head. "You never change."

"Nope, I never change. I'm still the same good old me. Everything still measures exactly the same."

Kathie Lee rolled her eyes. "Do you think women really want to hear that crap?"

I shook my head. "You know, you're swearing a lot. You didn't used to talk like that."

"Screw it." She sipped her coffee. "I've had so many people throw me over—not to mention you."

I looked down at the floor. I studied Kathie Lee's toenails. They were painted a sexy blood red. "Yeah, well, I know—"

"NO—you don't know. Otherwise you wouldn't be telling me about some chick you just met. What's the matter with you? Aren't you planning to grow up some day?"

"HEY." I glared at her. "I always told you what I thought. But for some reason—"

"Here we go again."

"No, look. You always liked guys who were a challenge. I have one moment of talking to some girl and you get all angry."

24

"Oh, please."

"It's true."

"God." She put her left hand to her forehead. "You have no respect for women."

"Yes I do."

"No you don't."

"Yes I do."

She shook her head. "This is so tedious. I'm not gonna get into this with you."

"But look—"

"No." She waved her hand in the air. "I can't do this. I'll talk to you later." She turned and walked away.

I Double Dare You

Whoopi and I were hanging out at Oprah's party up in the hills, sitting on a couch in the sunroom. We were sipping Blundetto champagne, laughing and talking. Whoopi had her hand on my knee. I took a sip of champagne and said, "You know what, baby, let's see how long we can go without talking."

Whoopi exploded with an incredulous laugh. "WHAT?"

"No really, baby, let's see how long we can sit here and not talk."

"Why?"

"I dunno. Just to do it."

"But why?"

"Well, let's see if we can do it. I'll bet you can't sit here for ten minutes without saying a word."

"Oh come on."

"I'm serious."

"But we're at a party. We're supposed to be talking."

"Exactly."

Whoopi shook her head. Her bracelets clicked around her wrists. She kissed me on the cheek. "You are so crazy—you know that?"

"I'm trying."

She took a sip of her champagne. "All right."

I took a sip of my champagne. "Okay, ten minutes. We'll use my watch."

"No, not ten minutes. That's too long."

"Okay, five."

"Done."

"All right—but we can drink champagne while we do it."

"Okay." Whoopi took another sip of her champagne. "But what are we betting?"

"Oh, right...umm... If I win, you have to go up to Aaron Spelling and kiss him on the lips and say, 'Baby, I've got a Melrose Place that's just waiting for your big 90210.'"

"WHAT?"

"Yup, that's what you gotta do."

"Come on?"

"I'm serious."

Whoopi took another sip of champagne. She paused. "All right. I can do that." She nodded to herself and giggled. She took another sip of champagne. "But if I win, you gotta go over to Sylvester Stallone and say, 'Sly, you have the brains of a twinkie.'"

"ARE YOU KIDDING?"

"Nope. If I win, you gotta walk right up to him and say, 'Sly, you make cheesy movies and you got the brain of a twinkie.'"

"I have to say all that?"

"Yup."

"Why?"

"'Cause you were complaining about him, like five minutes ago."

"But that's 'cause he started talkin' trash about Roseanne."

"So?"

"Yeah...all right." I raised my champagne glass. We clinked our champagne glasses. "Here, I'll count us in and we'll look at my watch."

"Okay."

"But you be ready to kiss Aaron Spelling."

"Fat chance."

"Yeah?"

"Yup."

"We'll see." I rolled up my sleeve and straightened my Rolex. "Ready?"

"Uh-huh."

I waited till the second hand reached the 12. "Okay... NOW."

I sat back on the couch, holding my champagne glass. Whoopi sat back against the couch. She exhaled softly.

A moment later, Heather Graham drifted into the room. Her lips glistened with red lipstick. She paused to adjust her mini-skirt. I took a long sip of my champagne and watched her. Heather smiled at us. "Hey, where'd you guys get the champagne? What I wouldn't give for some champagne right now."

I bolted out of my seat. "You can have mine." I handed her my champagne glass. "It's only about half-full. But mmm-hmm, it's delicious."

Whoopi jumped up from the couch. "AH-HAH—you talked."

I spun around. "Huh?"

Whoopi poked me in the chest. "You talked. You couldn't even wait thirty seconds."

"Oh." I shook my head. "No, no—that doesn't count. The bet was that I wouldn't talk to you."

"No, no—you said we couldn't TALK for five minutes."

"Right. We couldn't talk to each other."

"No, no—"

Heather looked from me to Whoopi. "What the hell are you guys talking about?"

Whoopi stepped in front of me. "Sister, what you see here is a man who can't keep his word. We had a bet that—"

I shook my head. "No, wait, wait—"

Whoopi pushed me away. "Check this out. We had a bet that we wouldn't talk for five minutes and if I won he'd go—"

"No, no, no. The bet was, we couldn't talk to each other."

"No, no..." Whoopi pushed me away again. She looked at Heather. "It's like this. He lost the bet and now he's trying to talk his way out of it."

Heather frowned. "What a pig."

"Oh, come on."

Whoopi nodded. "It's true. He can't keep his word."

I tried to grab her arm. "I always keep my word."

"Not this time."

"Oh come on..."

Heather turned to Whoopi. "What'd he bet?"

"Shoot, girl. You wanna know what he has to do?"

"Yeah." Heather smiled. Her lips were wet and shiny. "What's he gotta do?"

"Well..." Whoopi paused and downed the rest of her champagne. "He's gotta go up to Sly and say, 'Boy, you make cheesy movies 'cause you're dumb as a twinkie.'"

"No, no—it wasn't exactly that..."

Heather squinted at me. "You have to walk up to Sylvester Stallone and say that?"

I shook my head. "No, it's not like that."

Whoopi threw up her hands. "See what I'm talkin' 'bout, sister? He's just a boy—he's a scared boy. He can't keep his word."

Heather frowned. "God, I hate men. They're so weak. I like guys with strong you-know-whats."

Whoopi laughed. "I hear what you're saying."

I took back my glass of champagne from Heather. I gulped down the little bit that was left. "I've got guts."

"No you don't."

"Yes I do."

"No you don't."

I looked from Whoopi to Heather. "So what are you beautiful ladies telling me—I gotta go tell Sly he's an idiot?"

They both nodded, "Yup."

"Jesus." I kicked the toe of my shoe against the floor. "He'll twist me into little pretzel bits."

Whoopi waved her hand in the air. "Then you should pray to the Lord for some good luck."

"God..." I put my hand to my head. "I'm a condemned man." I stared at the floor.

Heather put her arm around me. "Oh, don't be sad. I'll go and visit you in the hospital."

"You will?"

"Sure." She looked at Whoopi for a moment. "We both will—won't we?"

Whoopi nodded. "Yup."

I looked at Heather. She had beautiful, sparkling eyes. "Really?"

"Yes. I'll come and see you. I'll read to you. I'll give you sponge baths."

My hands began to tremble. "Wait, wait, I'm starting to have palpitations. Could you repeat that last bit?"

Heather laughed. She poked my arm. "Oh, stop. You're gonna be fine."

"I know, I know. It's just that the sponge bath thing—my God..."

Whoopi threw up her hands. "The boy is just so helpless."

Heather smiled. I raised my empty champagne glass. "Let's get more champagne. Then we'll go talk to Sly."

"All right."

We started to walk out to the back veranda. We passed David Lane and Drew Barrymore. They were deep in private conversation. Whoopi grabbed my arm. "By the way, sailor boy, you're talking to Sly by yourself. Don't you mention my name."

"Come on..."

"I'm serious."

I nodded my head. "All right..."

We stepped out onto the veranda and crossed over to the bar. My friend Joe Guerriero was leaning against the bar, sipping a glass of wine. He saw me and grinned. "Stevie—hey...let me tell you something...it's all about timing, baby."

I nodded. "I hear that, Joe-Joe."

Joe picked up his glass of wine and drifted away. Heather looked at me. "Who the hell was that?"

"I think I did an audition with him once."

"Oh..."

I turned to the bartender. "Three champagnes, please—two for these lovely ladies, of course." Whoopi rolled her eyes. The bartender poured us each a champagne. I tipped him a $10 bill. Then we walked down the back steps to the courtyard.

Heather took my arm. "You know, you've got a lot of guts."

I squeezed her shoulder. "Baby, I've got lots of things."

She laughed. "You are such a cheeseball, you know that?"

"But you love me."

"Come on? I don't even know you."

"Really?"

"I just met you."

"All right. I'm gonna give you two days." I held up two fingers.

"Two days for what?"

I took a sip of my champagne. "In two days you're gonna be begging everyone you know for my phone number."

"Oh... right. Of course I will."

Whoopi tapped us on the shoulder. "Look, there's Sly."

I looked. Sly was standing near the swimming pool, talking with Bruce Willis, James Coburn, and James Caan. He was wearing a black suit, black pants, a white shirt. Instead of a tie, he had a bolo cinched around his neck.

"Oh, jeez..."

"Come on, don't back down on us now. This is gonna be funny."

"Who's gonna be laughing?"

Heather squeezed my arm. She smiled and looked into my eyes. "Come on. Be my big strong man."

"Oh, jeez." I gulped down my champagne. "This is like..."

"Here, give me your champagne glass."

I gulped down the last of my champagne. Then I handed my glass to Whoopi. I glanced at Sly. "All right. See you on the other side."

Whoopi pushed me. "Oh, you'll be fine. Stop it."

"All right."

Whoopi patted me on the back. I set off for Sly and his friends.

I rounded the swimming pool and walked up to Sly and his gang. They were standing in a narrow circle, smoking cigars and drinking whiskey. James Caan was saying, "Yeah, but Randy Newman speaks to the common man. That Reilly guy—he's more of a hippie. I can't dig his stuff. I wouldn't want my kids hearing that crap."

"Damn right," said James Coburn.

"Yeah," said Bruce Willis.

I stepped up to Sly. His back was toward me. All I could see was the enormous, tight girth of his broad sport coat. I tapped him on the shoulder.

"Hey, Sly—if you have a second..."

He turned around and faced me. He clenched his jaw and stared at me. "Yeah?"

"I was hoping you'd have a moment. I'm supposed to pass a message to you."

"Make it quick."

"Well, if you have a second, maybe we could step over there..."

"No. What's the message?"

"Well, there's no need to interrupt your whole conversation. We could talk over there."

"Look pal, speak your peace already."

Bruce Willis pointed at me. "Yeah. Whatever you gotta say to him, you can say to us."

Sly nodded. "Right."

"Well then...it goes like this...it seems I agreed to make the following observation and pass it along to you."

I paused. They were all staring at me. I glanced around quickly. Whoopi and Heather were watching from a nearby table.

"Okay, here goes. You see, Sly, you make cheesy movies and you have the brain of a twinkie."

I held my breath. Sly squinted at me.

"What did you say?"

"Well, I can repeat the message if you want—"

Sly pushed me hard in the chest. I stumbled backward. He pointed at me. "You got some kind of problem, pal? You wanna start something in front of my friends?"

I pointed at Sly. "Hey, soul brother, don't push me. It's just a joke."

"What the hell do you—"

Bruce Willis grabbed Sly's shoulder. "Let me kick his ass, Sly. You want me to kick his ass?"

Sly never took his eyes off me. "You wanna go right now, pal—right here?"

"Actually Sly, I don't know if that's such a good idea. I'm pretty much a bad-ass myself. I dunno if we need to start fighting, 'cause I'll get some shots in, I'll tell you that. But let's talk about it. If I say, 'You make cheesy movies,' I'm just—"

Suddenly James Caan stepped in front of me. He pointed his cigar at me. "You're friends with Burt, right?"

I nodded. "Yeah."

He shook his head. "Then why are you pissing off Sly?"

"It was a joke. I was supposed to walk up to Sly and tell him—"

"Who told you?"

"Who told me what?"

Sly grabbed the front of my sport jacket. "Who told you I make cheesy movies?"

"Well, no one—I mean, anyone who goes to the movies—"

Sly raised his fist. "I oughta pound you—"

James Caan grabbed Sly's arm. "Hey, Sly—easy. Take it easy."

"You hear what he said to me?"

James Caan pushed Sly away from me. "Look, Sly, back off. It's not worth it."

"Damn."

Sly shoved me again, then stepped back. He pointed at me. "You better watch it, pal."

A crowd had begun to gather. James Coburn stumbled between us. He took a swig of his whiskey. "You know what? There's only one way to settle this. I got gloves in the trunk. You guys're gonna put 'em on. You're gonna box." He took another swig of his whiskey. "It's the only way to settle this thing."

"Yeah," Bruce Willis shouted.

Just then, Oprah ran up to us. She was livid. "Hey—what the hell's going on here?" She glanced quickly from me to Sly to Bruce. "This is supposed to be a party. What the hell are you doing?"

Sly pointed at me. "He started it. He came over here and started making fun of me."

Oprah squinted at Sly. "What?"

"He did it. He started the whole thing."

"He did—did he?"

"Yeah."

"Well—so what?"

"He said I make cheesy movies."

"You do make cheesy movies."

"Yeah, but Oprah—I mean, I don't give a damn if you say that—"

Oprah glared at Sly. Her eyes narrowed. She pointed a finger in Sly's face. "Don't-you-ever-use-profanity-with-me. You hear me?"

Sly looked down at the ground. "No, no, I'm sorry. I just meant—"

"I know what you meant." She turned and stared at me. "So what's your problem?"

I put up my hands in a gesture of innocence. "Look, Oprah, baby, it's not what you—"

Oprah squinted at me. "What'd you call me?"

"Oprah—I mean, that's your name, right?"

"You called me 'baby.'"

"I call everybody 'baby.'" I looked around, searching for agreement from the crowd.

Oprah pointed a finger in my face. "If you know what's good for you, you'll never call me 'baby' again. Is that clear?"

"Sure thing, b—" I had to stop myself. I nodded. "Sure. Anything you say."

Bruce Willis gestured at Oprah. "Hey, Oprah, if I can just say something. I mean, this guy came up to us and—"

Oprah pointed at Bruce Willis. "Don't open your mouth again."

"I'm just trying to explain—"

"I don't want to hear it." Oprah looked around at the assembled crowd. "All right, everybody. Let's go back to having a party. Just forget about this. Let's all have a good time." She put her hands on her hips. "And somebody find Steadman. Tell him I want a glass of wine. I'll be in my office." She walked off.

I glanced around at everyone. Heather and Whoopi were watching me. I glanced at Sly, then walked away.

I started to walk back to the bar. After a moment, Heather caught up with me. She grabbed my arm. "You were so brave. I couldn't believe it."

I nodded. "That's how you gotta be, baby. It's a tough world out there. You can't let—"

Heather grabbed my arm. "Let's go hang out with Whoopi. We'll get some drinks."

"Sure thing, baby." We headed off to the bar.

Winona, Part 1

It was Christmas Day and I was sitting in my red Hyundai, stopped at a traffic light on Sunset. A black BMW pulled up next to me. I looked over and saw Winona Ryder sitting behind the steering wheel. Her window was open. I waved to her.

"Winona, baby, I love you. Let's get lunch."

Winona glanced at me quickly, then looked away.

I leaned out my window. "Listen, Winona, you and I need to do a project together. We need a good vehicle. Something from the heart, you know?"

She turned to me quickly. "Uhh, thanks...no."

I smiled. "Well, listen, I've seen all your work. Great stuff, beautiful stuff. You and I should do a drama together. Something people can relate to."

She ignored me, but I was on a roll. "People are tired of the big action stuff, you know, like Aliens 4, Rocky 5. All that junk. They want something more romantic. Like 'Officer and a Gentle—'"

Winona turned to me sharply. "Hey, I was in Aliens 4."

I paused. I looked at her. "Oh, well, baby...I loved Aliens 4."

The light turned green. Winona's car raced off in a screech of tires.

Slowhand on a Slow Night

I was leaving the Hollywood Roosevelt one night when I ran into Eric Clapton. He was wearing a brown leather jacket, jeans, and boots. A bellhop was trying to flag down a cab for him. I hurried over to shake his hand.

"Eric, baby, great to have you in L.A."

Clapton looked up at me. "I'm sorry. Do I know you?"

I smiled and reached to shake his hand. "Maybe not. I'm a huge fan. I buy all your records. Even the new ones."

Clapton shook my hand quickly. "Thanks." He dropped my hand.

I slapped him on the back. "Listen, you are the best guitar player in the world. I bet you hear that all the time, right?"

Clapton motioned to the bellhop. "Any luck on that taxi?"

The bellhop was tooting his taxi whistle. He glanced quickly at Clapton. "Any moment, sir."

I looked at Clapton. "You need a ride somewhere? I'm parked right over there."

Clapton shook his head. "No thanks."

I patted him on the shoulder. "It's no problem, man. Anything for a fellow artist."

Clapton squinted at me. "You're a musician?"

"Well, not any more. But let me tell you, I know talent. You are the greatest guitar player ever. You could pour beer on a guitar and it would sound great. Anything you do man, let me tell you—"

Suddenly a cab rolled up to the curb. The bellhop pulled open the door. Clapton climbed into the cab, shut the door, and was gone. I turned to the bellhop. "Did you see that, man? Eric Clapton."

The porter started to walk back into the lobby. "Uhh...yeah, sure."

I nodded and walked out to my Hyundai.

Chips, Dips, Chains, Whips

A week later, I went to Regis' birthday bash at Fro-Zen. It was a buffet sushi party. I was drinking sake with David Duchovny and Joe Guerriero. We were discussing Kathie Lee Gifford's new soul album, 'I Honestly Love You,' which was playing over the restaurant's sound system. Joe was just remarking that Kathie Lee's voice sounded "wetter than paint" when someone tapped me on the shoulder. I spun around. It was Regis. He squinted at me. "You have a second?"

"Sure, sure." I nodded at him and turned to Joe and David. I held up my glass of sake and toasted them. "Excuse me, fellas."

"Sure thing."

"Yeah."

I followed Regis to a quiet corner near the bar. He was sipping a martini. He gestured at a stack of stereo speakers in the corner of the room. Kathie Lee was scatting doo-wop phrases. He pointed at one of the speakers and shook his head. "No matter where I go, I can't get away from this crap."

I nodded gravely. "I hear you, man."

He took a sip of his martini. "I wanna talk to you a moment."

"Sure, Reeg."

"Listen, Barbra's Streisand's here and she really likes you..."

"Oh, man, not this..." I shook my head.

"Listen to me. She really likes you. She met you at Molod's or something and—"

"Aww, Reeg—"

He poked me in the shoulder. "Let me finish, okay?

I nodded. "All right."

Regis looked at his martini for a moment. He stirred his olive. "Somehow, she's really fallen for you. I don't know why. But she really likes you. And since she's here, I want her to have a good time."

He stared at me for a moment, waiting for me to say something. I nodded at him. "So what do you want me to do?"

"Go talk to her. Be nice to her. Show her a good time."

"But she's not my type, man."

"She's a sweet girl."

"I don't want a sweet girl."

"Look, just do me a favor. Go have a drink with her."

"Aww, Reeg. Come on…"

Regis pointed his finger at me. "Go-have-a-drink-with-her."

I kicked my shoe on the floor. "All right..." I sighed. "Fine. I'll go talk to her."

"That's the spirit."

I downed the rest of my sake and exhaled. "Where is she?"

"Right over there." He pointed to the other side of the bar.

I looked over and saw Barbra standing near the bar. She was wearing a long brown evening dress and a string of pearls. I nodded to Regis. "All right. Here goes."

Regis patted me on the back. "Go to it."

I walked up to the bar, near where Barbra was standing. I leaned toward the bartender and ordered a double-sake. Almost instantly, Barbra spotted me. She hurried over and grabbed my arms. Her nose brushed my ear as she gave me a kiss on the cheek. She squeezed my shoulders. "Hi darling. How are you?"

I smiled. "Fine, baby. How are you?"

"Just terrific. Just wonderful."

"Great. I'm glad to hear that."

The bartender handed me a double-sake. I put a $5 bill in his tip jar. I turned to Barbra. "Can I get you a drink?"

"Oh, no. I don't drink."

"Oh."

I took a long hit of my sake. It was nice and warm, the way I liked it. Barbra looked at the sake for a moment, then looked at me. She touched my arm. "So what's new with you? You look great."

I took another hit of the sake. "Yeah, you know...Some auditions and things. Working on a couple of projects. You know, the usual."

Barbra smiled. She was staring into my eyes. "That's wonderful. I mean, you are so talented. Anything you do must be grand."

"Yeah, you know...Just working it."

She touched my arm again. "Let's take a seat." She gestured toward the stereo speakers. "I don't want to have to shout over this noise."

"It's Kathie Lee."

"Whatever."

I nodded. "All right." I slugged down the rest of my sake and put the glass on the bar. I started to wave to the bartender. "Let me just get another drink..."

Barbra grabbed my arm. "No. I don't want to share you with a drink."

"But, baby..."

She tightened her grip. "Come on." She began pulling me toward one of the small tables in the back corner. I made a last glance for the bartender. But Barbra was tugging my arm. I gave up and followed her to an empty table.

A small orange candle was glowing in a glass cup at the side of the table. We sat down. Barbra looked into my eyes again. "The last time I saw you, we were having dinner with Burt and Loni."

"I remember."

"You gave me the tie you were wearing."

"I did?"

"Yes."

I lifted my hand to take a hit of sake. But there was no glass in my hand. I looked at my empty hand for a moment. Barbra reached across the table and took my hand. She looked into my eyes. "I kept hoping we'd run into each other."

"Really?"

She held my hand tightly. "Yes."

"Well, that's great." I nodded and looked away. "Yeah."

I felt Barbra staring at me. I nodded and tried to think of something to say: "So...yeah...what've you been doing with yourself?"

Barbra smiled. She touched my fingers. "Mostly yoga. Some reading. That kind of thing."

"Yeah."

Suddenly Barbra's cell phone rang. She let go of my hand and reached into her purse. She flipped on the cell.

"Yes?...Uh-huh...Yes, I ordered it...Oh, well please tell Alia to sign for it, okay?...Just leave it in the kitchen...Okay...Grazie. Ciao." She closed her phone and stuck it back in her bag. She turned back to me. "Where were we?"

"I don't know."

I was thinking of a warm sake. But Barbra was looking at me. After a moment, I stumbled for something to say. "Umm...what was the phone call?"

She waved her hand dismissively. "Ohh, just some leather I ordered."

"Really?"

"Yeah. It's nothing."

"Leather, like for what? Like furniture or something?"

She smiled to herself. "Well...not exactly."

"I like leather."

"Me, too."

"Yeah, leather's cool."

Barbra smiled. She looked at the table. "Leather's not always cool. Sometimes it's hot."

I paused. "Umm, 'leather's hot'...how's that, baby?"

Barbra reached across the table and took my hand again. "If you wrap leather tight enough, it can start to sweat."

I nodded my head. "Yeah...I guess that's possible. There's, like, water vapor trapped in it, or something..."

Barbra shook her head. "No. It depends on who you wrap the leather around."

"Oh."

She squeezed my hand. "It's like whip cream. You spray it on someone and it starts to melt. Sometimes you have to act quickly." She looked at me.

I nodded. "What do you do when it melts?"

"I don't let it melt."

She was staring at me. I stared back. "How do you keep it from melting?"

She paused, then licked her lips.

I squinted at her. "I don't get it."

She licked her lips again.

I nodded. "Oh..."

Suddenly my heart started to beat faster. I felt a tiny bead of sweat appear on my forehead.

Barbra grinned. "But whip cream's only good if you have an hour or so."

"Yeah."

"That's why I prefer candle wax."

"Yeah."

"Or tree cuffs."

"Tree cuffs?"

"Tree handcuffs."

"Oh." I leaned forward. "French or Thai?"

"Thai. Always Thai."

A drop of sweat rolled down the side of my face. I looked into Barbra's eyes. "You like radiators?"

Barbra's body suddenly convulsed in a spasm. "Unhh..." She blinked her eyes. "I love them."

"What about carpet fibers?"

She leaned forward. Her breasts hovered above the edge of the table. "Only synthetic."

I felt myself shudder.

Barbra let go of my hand. She reached under the table and began rubbing my thigh. She stared into my eyes. "Do you like mirrors?"

"Only in the bathroom and on the ceiling."

Barbra's fingernails dug into my leg. "And towels?"

"Rolled-up like a tube."

Barbra stood up. My heart was pounding. I pressed my hand against my chest. She leaned over me. "You don't use pillows do you?"

"NEVER."

Barbra stepped away from the table. "Let's go."

I jumped up, almost knocking over my chair. We hurried to the front door.

Winona, Part 2

Just after New Year's I went to a party at Aaron Spelling's house in the Hills. It was a crowded party. I saw the producer Vin Blunno talking with David Lane and Drew Barrymore. Drew was giving David a neck rub. I drifted past them and said hello. Then I walked over to the bar and ordered a champagne.

I picked up my champagne and strolled out toward the balcony. Suddenly Sandra Bullock darted in front of me, almost knocking over my champagne.

"Whoah, Sandy..."

"WHAT?"

"My champagne, baby. You gotta be careful."

Sandra gave me a quick look and hurried away. She ducked into a nearby bathroom and locked the door.

I stepped out onto the balcony and looked out at Los Angeles. Smog had covered most of the city. I couldn't see the ocean. At that moment, a beautiful blonde walked up next to me. I smiled at her and gestured with my champagne.

"Beautiful night."

The blonde sipped some of her champagne. "I guess so."

I looked at her for a moment. The way she held her chin seemed familiar. There was something about her profile... Suddenly I recognized her. Terri Nunn, the lead singer of Berlin.

"Oh wow, Terri, baby—how are you?"

She nodded slowly and took a sip of champagne. "Fine."

I shook her hand. "I'm a big fan. You are just awesome."

"Thanks."

"So, baby, tell me, how's the music life?"

Terri inspected her champagne for a moment. "Mmm, this is good stuff..."

I took a sip. "Yeah."

She looked at me. "I'm sorry...what were you saying?"

"Oh, you know, just wondering about you." I gave her my big smile, the one that had reeled in Barbra Streisand. "I mean, you are just so fine. You are one beautiful lady. And your eyes... If I could buy all the stars in the sky—"

"Enough, enough." She waved her hand at me. "I hate all this silly talk."

I smiled. "Sure, baby. It's just that, you know, you're so graceful and all."

"Thanks."

Terri looked out at the twinkling lights of the city. She took a sip of champagne. "This is a nice view."

"Yeah."

She paused. "But you know, I really don't like this town. I don't enjoy parties like this."

"Oh, baby, don't say that."

"I mean this whole place..." She gestured at the city with her hand. "The only good thing is that I met my husband here."

"You're married?"

"Engaged."

I nodded. "Oh."

Terri shivered for a moment. She took a sip of her champagne. "All the men here...all they talk about are their big wallets."

I shook my head. "Not me, baby."

She laughed. "I like you. You're like a big clown. And you're genuine. I like that."

"Yeah, baby."

She held up her champagne glass. "Here's to the good men."

"Right on."

We clinked our glasses.

Just at that moment, Winona Ryder drifted by. She spotted Terri. "Oh my God, Terri Nunn. Wow." She ran up to us. "Oh my God. I-am-such-a-Berlin-fan."

Terri winked at me and turned to Winona. "Thanks."

Winona reached out and shook Terri's hand. "Wow, I mean, my friends and I thought you were such a great artist. Just as a woman and all. I mean, you are so beautiful. You have such class."

"Thank you."

"I mean, like, look at MTV and the role of women and everything. You are so awesome. You transcended all the stereotypes, you know?"

Terri smiled. She took a sip of her champagne and nodded. "What was your favorite Berlin record?"

"Oh, well, I liked them all. I had a poster of you that was so expressive. You seemed to capture the whole post-modern thing, you know—like sort of—"

Terri put up her hand. "Whoah...slow down."

Winona smiled bashfully. "Sorry, I'm just a little excited."

Terri patted Winona on the arm. "That's all right." She took a sip of her champagne. "What's your name?"

Winona froze. She looked at Terri blankly. Her mouth opened, but no sound came out.

I put my arm around Winona's shoulder and turned to Terri. "Terri, baby, this is the lovely and the talented Winona Ryder."

Winona ignored me. She smiled at Terri. "Are you playing in town? I'd love to see you."

Terri took a sip of her champagne. "We played last night, actually...But listen, your name's familiar..."

I smiled. "Yes, Winona was in Aliens 4."

Terri sputtered. "Aliens 4?"

Winona looked from me to Terri. "Uh...yeah..."

Terri spit out part of her champagne. "Oh my God, that's..." She began to cough.

I squinted at Terri. "Baby, are you all right? Do you need some water?"

"—Aliens 4?"

"Yeah."

"Oh my God..." She seemed to be choking. "...That's...horrible..."

I tried to pat her on the back. "Baby, are you okay?"

Winona looked from me to Terri. "Uhh..."

I patted Terri's back. After a moment, she seemed to catch her breath. I looked at her. "Are you okay, baby?"

She coughed lightly. "Yeah."

I put my arm around her. "Maybe we should get some more champagne?..."

She nodded and coughed. "Yes...all right."

Winona looked from me to Terri. "I'm sorry...I didn't—"

I ignored her and led Terri back into the main room. We headed for the bar.

In Defense of Keanu Reeves

The next day, I bumped into Keanu Reeves outside Panne Chocolat in Hollywood. I hadn't seen him since we'd worked on 'Speed'; I was the third SWAT team cop in the subway during the final chase scene. On this particular afternoon, I'd just left Larry's World of Protein Shakes after picking up a Soy-Guava Muscle Builder. Keanu and I were both trying to park our cars in the same spot along Franklin. He started to inch his Mercedes in front of my Hyundai. I leaned my head out the window.

"Hey Keanu—I'm parking here."

"Dude, I was here first."

"No you weren't."

"Yes I was."

I took a sip of my protein shake and climbed out of my car. "Look, you know I've always respected you. I love 'Point Break' and all. But I'm tellin' you, I was already backing into that spot."

"No you weren't, dude."

"Yes I was. I had my reverse light on."

"But you didn't have your signal on."

"It doesn't matter."

I paused and took a sip of my protein shake. Keanu looked at the shake. He pointed at it. "Dude, is that a Larry's shake?"

"Yup."

"Ahh, that's good stuff."

"Yeah."

Keanu smiled. "Anyone who's into protein shakes is all right with me." He gave me a funny look and repeated himself: "Anyone who's into protein shakes is all right with me."

Suddenly I felt light-headed. I tried to look at Keanu, but he was gesturing with his hand. He smiled at me. "This isn't the parking spot you're looking for."

I nodded. "This isn't the parking spot I'm looking for..."

"You're about to drive away."

"I'm about to drive away," I repeated.

"Keanu Reeves is a great actor."

"Keanu Reeves is a great actor..."

"Move along."

"Yeah..."

I smiled, got in my car, and drove away.

Sometimes You're The Bug, Sometimes You're the Windshield

I went to Paramount to audition for the role of second-bodyguard-with-dialogue in the upcoming feature, 'The Oprah Winfrey Story.' After my screen test, I stopped at the snack stand for a cup of coffee. It was late afternoon and the place was empty except for a beautiful dark-haired girl working behind the counter. As I walked up to her she gave me a big smile.

I grinned at her. "Hi, baby."

"Hi."

"Let me have a coffee."

She nodded and began to pour coffee into a styrofoam cup. "Cream and sugar?"

"Just sugar."

She smiled to herself. "I bet you like a lot of sugar."

"Yeah, baby. Lay it on me."

She laughed and began spooning sugar into my cup. "You know, I loved 'Article 99.'"

"What's that?"

"I thought you were fabulous."

I put a hand to my chest. "I am fabulous."

She grinned. "No, I mean you were fabulous...in 'Article 99.'"

I looked at her. "Baby, I wasn't in 'Article 99.'"

She stopped spooning sugar. "Aren't you Ray Liotta?"

"No."

"Oh." She stopped smiling. She put a top on my coffee cup. "That's a dollar-eighty."

I handed her $2 and took my coffee. As I walked out to the parking lot, I heard her drop the 20 cents change into her tip jar.

Target Practice

Later in the week, I ran into Rosie O'Donnell at Brizendine's. She was standing in the Roxy Room, throwing darts at a picture of Howard Stern. I drifted by, holding a Bailey's-on-the-rocks. I glanced at the dartboard, then turned to Rosie.

"Ouch, baby. That's gotta hurt."

Rosie stopped throwing darts. She squinted at me. "Did you just call me 'baby?'"

I took a sip of my Bailey's. "Yeah, I think so."

"Well, don't ever do it again."

"Baby, I'm sorry. Let me make it up to you."

Rosie pointed a finger at me. "I just told you NOT to call me 'BABY.'"

I waved my drink in the air. "Sure, sure, let me make it up to you. Let's go back to my place. We'll have a beer. Have a good time."

Rosie threw the rest of her darts. She stepped over to the dartboard and began removing them from the picture of Howard Stern. "No thanks." She stepped back and began throwing darts again.

I nodded and took a sip of my Bailey's. "All right. Can't say I didn't try."

Rosie kept throwing her darts. "No you can't."

"Okay..." I took another sip of my Bailey's and drifted away.

American Stars and Bars

Whoopi and I were standing at the bar outside the Grand Ballroom of the Beverly Wilshire Hotel. It was a gala night and we were attending a charity event for the American Spinal Research Marathon. The bar was crowded with people. Whoopi was wearing a silver dress; I looked great in my tux.

I stepped up to the bar. The bartender squinted at me. "Another double-vodka?"

"Lay it on me, baby."

Whoopi poked me in the ribs. "This is your last one, okay?"

I nodded slowly. "All right."

The bartender handed me my drink. I thanked him and put a $5 bill in his tip jar. Whoopi gave me a kiss on the cheek. "I'm going to the ladies room."

"Meet you back at the table?"

"Okay."

I took a sip of my drink. Whoopi walked off through the crowd. I watched her give a quick hug to Anjelica Huston. Then I turned and walked toward the ballroom. I took a sip of my drink and bumped into the producer Phil DeGuere. I gestured with my drink, "Hey Phil."

Phil grinned, "Hey man..."

I stepped through the entranceway to the ballroom and stumbled across Geraldo Rivera. He was surrounded by a TV crew. They were preparing to interview Keanu Reeves. The TV crew had hoisted a camera into place. Suddenly a spotlight switched on. Geraldo and Keanu were bathed in bright light. I took a sip of my drink and walked over to Geraldo.

Geraldo gripped a microphone and shouted over the noise of the room. "We're LIVE with Mr. Hollywood himself, Keanu Reeves. He's about to be raffled off for the American Spinal Research Bachelor Contest."

Keanu grinned. Geraldo smiled and turned to Keanu. "You've made some very memorable films: 'The Matrix,' 'Bill and Ted,' 'Johnny Mnemonic'..."

"Don't forget 'Speed,'" I said from off-camera.

Geraldo glanced at me quickly and turned back to Keanu. "...And of course, 'Speed.'"

Keanu nodded. "Right."

Geraldo switched the microphone to his other hand. "Now tonight you're here for a good cause."

"That's right."

I took a sip of my drink and stepped next to Geraldo. I put my hand on his shoulder. "Hey Geraldo...can I just say that my buddy Keanu was tremendous in 'Speed.' Just tremendous."

Geraldo stared at me. "Uhh, thanks." He turned back to Keanu. "I guess some people are very fond of 'Speed.'"

Keanu shrugged. "Yeah."

I patted Geraldo on the back. "You know, I'm tired of people saying that Keanu talks funny, like he tries to make his voice sound deeper and all that." I smiled at the camera. "Keanu is better than DeNiro, better than Redford, better than Nicholson—"

Geraldo nodded quickly. "Yes, okay, thanks." He tried to pull away from me.

I kept smiling. "And 'Sweet November'—what a masterpiece...Did you see it?"

Geraldo paused. He stared at the camera blankly. "Uhhh..."

I nudged him. "It's a masterpiece, right?"

Geraldo looked at me. "Well, maybe not a masterpiece, but..."

Suddenly two security men pushed me away from Geraldo. I clutched my drink and pulled away from them. I drifted back into the crowd.

A Real Meatball

The next weekend, I flew up to San Francisco to film a scene in Eddie Murphy's 'Metro II. The night after I arrived, I had dinner with Danny Glover at Il Borgo. We were sitting at a window table, downing glass after glass of merlot.

Danny was emptying the bottle of wine into his glass. He called to the owner, Sergio, for another bottle. As Sergio was fetching a second merlot, Danny pointed a finger at me. "I'm paying for the wine."

"Why?"

"'Cause I want the good stuff. You always get cheap wine and then I wake up with a headache the next day."

"Then don't look in the mirror."

Danny doubled over with laughter. "DAMN—'Don't look in the mirror'—AH-HAH-HAH..."

When he finished laughing, I said, "Okay. You get the wine and I'll buy dinner."

"All right."

Sergio brought us another bottle. He uncorked it and poured a glass for each of us. Just then, Jennifer Aniston and her entourage walked into the restaurant. I looked up and saw light glinting off her long, golden hair. A hush fell over the restaurant; everyone stared at her.

Sergio hurried over to greet Jennifer. "Welcome, welcome. Please...right this way..." He took Jennifer's coat and began to lead Jennifer and her group past our table.

As Jennifer drifted past our table, I took a quick sip of wine and stood up. "Hey, Jen?...Jen?..."

Jennifer paused. "Yes?"

"Listen, what did the fly say when it got hit with the fly swatter?"

"Umm...I don't know."

I grinned at her. "Nothing. Flies can't talk."

Instantly, Danny Glover cracked up. "AH-HAH-HAH..." He grabbed his stomach. "Oh, Jesus, that's a good one... 'Flies can't talk'—AH-HAH-HAH..."

Jennifer squinted at us for a moment. I smiled at her. "No, seriously baby, I love your work. 'Friends' is the best show on TV. I mean, I know everyone thinks 'Seinfeld' is a lot better, but—"

"Thanks."

Jennifer glanced at Danny, who was clutching his chest, moaning, "Oh, Christ...'Flies can't talk'..."

She turned away abruptly. But as she did, her long hair whipped across my face. Some of it brushed sharply against my eye. For a moment, I felt blinded. My wineglass slipped out of my hand and fell against her blouse. Jennifer grabbed for the wineglass.

I tried to catch the wineglass. But it bounced off of Jennifer's chest and shattered on the floor. She wheeled around. "HEY!!"

I put up my hands in protest. "Baby, I'm sorry. It was an accident."

Sergio ran up to us. "What happened?"

I tried to explain. "I'm really sorry. It was an accident. I spilled some wine on Jennifer Aniston's dress."

Sergio turned to Jennifer. "Jennifer Aniston?"

"Yes."

"The Jennifer Aniston on the show 'Friends.'"

She nodded. "Yes."

Sergio frowned. "My God. What an awful show. That's the worst show on TV."

I turned to Sergio. "Well, hold on. Jennifer's been in all kinds of things. I mean, before 'Friends,' she was on 'Ferris Bueller.'"

Sergio looked at me blankly. "There was a TV show of 'Ferris Bueller?'"

"Yeah. Like, four or five years after the movie."

Sergio wobbled. His face turned white. "My God...that's...horrible."

I looked at him. "Aww, don't say that..."

Sergio turned to Jennifer. "I want you out of my restaurant right now."

"But..."

"Right now."

Jennifer pointed at me. "He spilled wine on me—"

"LEAVE."

Jennifer looked down at the floor. "All right." She and her entourage began to walk to the door.

I patted Sergio on the arm. "Sorry about the mess."

"No problem. I'll bring you another bottle."

"Thanks, man."

I walked back to the table. Danny Glover was still laughing: "'Flies can't talk'—AH-HAH-HAH..." I sat down and grinned at Danny. We continued to drink wine.

God, Part 1

The morning after I got back to L.A., I got a phone call from my agent. He was calling to tell me that the scene I'd shot with Eddie Murphy in 'Metro II' had been scrapped. I'd still receive my per diem pay, but the producers had decided to change the direction of the film; the scene I'd filmed wouldn't fit the revised storyline.

I hung up the phone. "DAMNIT."

I felt really bummed. It was the biggest speaking role I'd ever earned: three lines. It was more than I'd had when I worked with Keanu in 'Speed.' I was crushed. I kicked a shoe across the floor in disgust. It bounced off the wall and narrowly missed my stack of Britney CDs piled near the stereo.

I walked into the kitchen and reached for a Bud. I was about to crack one open when I had a sudden urge to go hiking in the hills. I couldn't explain it, but I suddenly knew that I should put the Bud back in the fridge, leave my condo, and drive over to Griffith Park.

I hurriedly tossed the Bud back in the fridge and put on my hiking boots. Then I climbed into my Hyundai and drove south on the 101 to Los Feliz. It was a warm, hazy day and the highway was unusually empty. In 20 minutes, I was parked near the Griffith Park Golf Course.

I locked up my Hyundai and set off for a walk. As soon as I began to trudge up the dirt path toward the water tower I felt better.

I climbed higher into the hills and passed hearty, red-barked trees and bushes. Birds were chirping. I looked out at the flat, orange landscape of downtown L.A. I felt exhilarated. But then I remembered that I'd been cut from 'Metro II.' My depression returned. I kicked a rock on the ground and watched it tumble off the trail. I thought of Sandra and Winona. When would I reach the big time? When would I get to co-star with one of them?

I muttered aloud, "When's it gonna happen?"

Suddenly I felt a huge gust of wind. There was a whistling in the trees. A blast of chilly air rushed through my hair. Instinctively I raised my hand to my face and, as I did, I suddenly saw God. He was hovering in front of me in a haze of white light. Somehow I knew that it was Him. He looked a lot like David Geffen, but his hair wasn't as curly.

"Oh my God..."

I squinted against the rushing air. God smiled at me. He said, "All things in time."

And then He disappeared. The rushing air faded away. I was left standing in the middle of the woods, my hand raised to my face. The sound of chirping birds returned.

I was vaguely stunned. I'd never seen God before. I couldn't believe it.

I turned and ran back to my car. I raced home to call my agent. He was my one true friend in L.A. I knew he'd want to hear what God had said.

When I got back to my condo, I rushed inside and dialed my agent. His voicemail answered. I said, "Hey, it's me. Call me."

Then I hung up the phone and cracked open a Bud. I sat down on my sofa and waited for my agent to call back.

God, Part 2

That night I went to a party for Tara Reid that was being held at Rey-Rey's. Everyone was drinking Fischl Valley Pinot Noir, served on the house. I downed a glass at the bar, then ordered another. I tipped the bartender and drifted off through the cocktail room.

I bumped into Shannon Doherty. She was talking to Andy Dick. As I walked past, I heard her say, "Did you know that a man's testosterone levels decline rapidly after the age of 35?"

I smiled at Shannon as I passed. "Not me, baby."

She turned and grinned at me. "Really?"

I nodded. "It's like I always say, where there's a pulse, there's a vibe."

Andy Dick gave me a funny look. "Well that's sure helpful to know."

"Yeah...I guess so..." I nodded and drifted away from them.

After a few minutes, I spotted the producer Vin Blunno. He was talking to my old friend Joe Guerriero.

"Hey guys."

"Hey."

I took a sip of my wine. Vin pointed at Joe. "Did you know that our friend Joe here has been keeping company with Faith Hill."

I turned to Joe. "Wow. That's great, man."

Joe sipped his wine. "I tell you, it's like I died and went to heaven."

"I hear that."

We all nodded and sipped our wine. I grinned and looked down at my shoes for a moment. "Hey...speaking of heaven...I think I saw God today."

Vin chuckled. "A few more glasses of this pinot and I think I'm gonna see God, too."

Joe began to cackle. "Ah-hah-hah-hah..."

I looked at both of them. "No, I'm serious. I was hiking in the hills and..."

Vin poked me. "Did you ask him which was better, red or white?"

"No, no..."

Joe was cackling, "Ah-hah-hah-hah..."

Vin continued. "Next time ask him where I can get my shirts pressed so they won't shrink."

"...Ah-hah-hah-hah..."

I looked at both of them. "I'm serious guys. I think God spoke to me."

Just at that moment, Joe's cell phone beeped. He flipped it open. "Joe-oe Guerriero?..."

Vin turned to me. "So, is God a man or a woman?"

"A man. He looks sort of like David Geffen."

Vin paused. "Hmm...I guess that's possible."

Joe was talking into his cell phone. "What?...What?...Oh, yeah...absolutely...okay...right...speak with you soon...bye..." He switched off his cell phone and looked at us. "Guess what?"

"What?"

"Spielberg wants me to read for 'Schindler's List II.'"

"You're kidding?"

"Nope."

"That's great."

"Yeah."

Joe nodded. "Yup. Steven Spielberg...They're gonna call me tomorrow."

"That's great."

Joe smiled. "Let's celebrate. I could use a good cab."

I looked at him. "You're leaving?"

Joe chuckled. "No, a good cabernet."

"Ohh.

Joe patted me on the back. "Let's get a drink. I'll introduce you to Faith."

"Okay."

We headed for the bar. Life was turning out pretty good: God and Faith Hill in the same day.

God, Part 3

I was driving home along Santa Monica Boulevard at around 5 pm the next afternoon. Suddenly God appeared in my front passenger's seat. I was startled. "OH LORD…"

God turned to me quickly and said, "There is a reason for Sandra Bullock." Then he disappeared in a great rush of wind.

I lost control of my Hyundai and swerved abruptly into the right lane. The car next to me honked violently. There was a sudden thud as I banged into the other car.

The car skidded for a moment. Then the driver regained control and slowed down. I noticed that it was a woman driver. She quickly skidded to a stop. I slowed down and pulled in behind her. I parked. My hands were shaking. I reached into the glove compartment for my insurance card.

God had chosen to visit me again. I felt badly shaken.

I climbed out of the car.

Judge Judy

As soon as I got home from my car accident, I called my agent to tell him what had happened. I explained how God had suddenly appeared in my car and made me swerve across the road. My agent listened silently for a moment, then said, "All right, here's what we're gonna do…we're gonna make you into the next Kato…"

He wanted me to go on the 'Judge Judy' show to settle the case. He said that it would be good publicity for my career. And, since God had caused the accident, it wasn't my fault. Legally, I could argue that it was an "act of God," which would mean I wasn't responsible for any damages.

My agent made a few phone calls and, two months later, I appeared on the show wearing a blue suit. I saw the woman whose car I'd hit. Her name was Marilena. I tried to talk to her before the show, but she walked away nervously.

As soon as the show began taping, Judge Judy entered the courtroom. The bailiff announced, "All rise." We stood up. After a moment, Judge Judy said to Marilena, "All right ma'am, tell me exactly what happened."

Marilena looked at Judge Judy. "Your honor, I was driving on the street and he—"

"Don't point to anyone, ma'am. Tell me exactly who 'he' is."

"Him—the defendant."

"Okay, continue."

Marilena swallowed nervously. "The defendant's car crash into mine. I didn't see it coming or nothing."

"I see. Then what."

"He hit me and dented my door. I hurt my neck. My husband says I—"

"Stick to the facts, ma'am. I don't want to hear anything your husband says. We call that hearsay. It's not relevant here. Comprende?"

"Yes, your honor."

"All right, continue."

Marilena shuffled some papers nervously. "I have the receipt for the repair of my car. I also went to a doctor about my neck—"

"Was your neck hurting before the accident?"

"No, your honor."

"Okay."

"And I have the note from the doctor that says my neck got hurt. I also have the receipt from the doctor."

Judge Judy turned to the bailiff. "Bailiff will please take the papers from the plaintiff."

"Yes, your honor." The bailiff stepped over and took the paperwork from Marilena. She handed it to him nervously. He walked over and handed it to Judge Judy. She put on her reading glasses and studied the various slips of paper. After a moment, she looked up at Marilena. "Do you have insurance?"

"Yes, your honor?"

"Then why are you suing through this court?"

Marilena looked down for a moment. "I went to the insurance but this man said it's not his fault. He made me go to court."

Judge Judy looked at me. "Is that right, sir?"

I gave Judge Judy a big smile. "Yes, Judge Judy."

Judge Judy frowned at me. "In this courtroom you'll address me as 'your honor.' Is that clear?"

I nodded. "Absolutely."

She paused for a moment. "This woman says you hit her car. Is that true?"

I nodded again. "Yes, your honor."

"So what's the problem?"

"It's not my fault, your honor."

"It's not your fault?"

"That's right."

Judge Judy turned to Marilena. "Did you have anything more to say?"

"He hit my car, your honor. I was only driving and his car come up and hit me."

Judge Judy put up her hand. "Okay, okay." She turned to me. "Sir, if it's not your fault, whose fault is it?"

"God, your honor."

Judge Judy rolled her eyes. Behind me I could hear members of the audience begin to laugh. I turned around to them and waved quickly.

Judge Judy cleared her throat. "Sir. Do not look at the courtroom. Look at me. Only at me. Understand?"

"Yes, your honor."

Judge Judy turned to the bailiff. "This is a new one."

The bailiff nodded his head. "Yes it is, your honor."

Judge Judy turned to me. "Okay sir. Why is God responsible?"

I smiled. "Well, he came into my car. Out of nowhere."

The audience began to laugh. Judy Judy scowled at them. "Everyone keep quiet. I ask the questions. I don't want to hear a peep out of anyone else." She paused, then looked at me. "Sir, you're telling me that God appeared in your car."

"Yes your honor."

"Well that's certainly an interesting story. And did he have the white hair and the flowing robes?"

"No, your honor."

Judge Judy nodded. "I see….and, what did he look like?"

"Sort of like David Geffen."

I could hear the audience chuckling. Judge Judy glared at them for a moment. Then she turned back to me. "He looked like David Geffen, the record producer?"

"Yes, your honor."

Judge Judy nodded. "Uh-huh. Then what?"

"He talked to me, your honor."

Judge Judy looked at the bailiff. "This is getting very interesting."

The bailiff nodded. He was grinning. "Yes your honor."

Judge Judy turned back to me. "And what did God say to you?"

I paused. "Well your honor, it was very brief. He said 'There is a reason for Sandra Bullock.'"

Behind me the audience was laughing. Judge Judy squinted at them. "I don't know if it'll do any good to remind this courtroom to remain absolutely quiet." She turned back to me. "So God talked to you, and that means you're not responsible for this traffic accident?"

I gave Judge Judy another smile. "Well, your honor, I was startled. I lost control of my car. Normally I'm a great driver."

"I see. It was God's fault."

"Right, your honor. It was an act of God."

Judge Judy shook her head. She looked at the bailiff. "This is the biggest load of baloney I've ever heard."

"But it really happened, your honor."

Judge Judy shook her head. "Sorry. I ain't buying it. This is a simple case. You hit her car, you pay for the damages." She rapped her gavel. "Judgement for the plaintiff, all costs. Case closed."

Judge Judy stood up and walked out of the courtroom. The bailiff was already saying, "All rise…"

After a moment I walked out of the courtroom. The show's reporter was waiting for me in the hallway. His hair was perfect. He waved to me and held up a microphone. "Tell me—what do you think of Judge Judy's verdict?"

I looked at the camera and smiled. "It was great. She's great."

He raised his eyebrows. "Really? Most people seem disappointed when they lose a case."

I shook my head. "Not me. I thought it was great working with Judy. She's got great presence. She's one of the strongest women in TV today."

He chuckled. "No one's ever talked about the judge like that before."

I smiled at the camera again. "What can I say? I'm a fan. I hope she does a feature soon. Maybe a comedy or something. You know—just to break out of the mold."

The reporter looked at me for a moment. "Uhh, yes…well, thanks for your time…"

"My pleasure."

The camera light switched off. I walked away.

Why Yes, I Am

I was walking down Hollywood Boulevard, wearing my big boots, when two girls stopped me. They were giggling and pointing at me.

"Oh my God. You're that guy."

"Oh my God. Wow."

I grinned. "Hello."

"Oh my God. Oh my God."

"Oh my God. You were in that commercial. Right?"

"Yes. That was me."

"Oh my God."

One of the girls started waving her hand back and forth. "Wow. This is so exciting." She tried to catch her breath. "And you were in 'Speed,' too."

I shook my head. "No, I was in 'Speed One.' The first one. The good one, with my buddy Keanu."

"Wow. You know Keanu?"

"We talk from time to time."

"Oh My God. Wow."

"What's he like?"

"He's terrific. He's a very skilled actor and a real professional. It's always great to work with him."

One of the girls pulled a journal out of her knapsack. "Can I have your autograph?"

The other girl nodded. "Me too."

I smiled at them. "Sure thing. I'd be happy, too." I took the journal and pen. "What's your name?"

"Candace."

I opened the journal and found a clean page. "Well, Candace, I want to inscribe this to you personally because I think you're terrific. You girls are terrific."

"Wow."

"Oh my God."

The other girl rummaged through her bag for a piece of paper.

"We found your picture on the Internet. That's how I knew you were in 'Speed.'"

"Well that's great."

"Yeah. And we looked for you in 'Speed' and I think we saw you right at the end, when they go running into the subway."

"That's right." I handed the journal back to the first girl. The second one handed me a scrap of paper. I began to scribble my name.

The girl looked at me. "You look different in person."

I handed back the scrap of paper. "You think so?"

She nodded. "Yeah. You looked kind of younger in the movie."

"Oh...well, that was the make-up. Keanu and I both used a bit of make-up in that scene. You know, all the fluorescent lights and all."

"Wow."

"Wow."

The first girl put her journal back in her bag. We stood there for a moment. I smiled at them. "How come you two ladies aren't in school today?"

They began to giggle. "It's July. We don't have school in the summer."

"Oh, right."

They giggled again. I laughed, too. "Well, what are you doing with the rest of your day?"

"Ummm—"

Suddenly the girls' mom came up behind them. "Candace. What are you doing?"

The girl pointed at me. "Look who it is, mom."

The mom grabbed both of the girls by the arm. "I told you, never talk to people you don't know. If someone looks strange—-"

"But mom—-"

"Come on." She gave me a quick look and started pulling the girls away.

"But mom—-"

"WE ARE LEAVING."

One of the girls looked back at me. "Bye."

I waved goodbye.

The Producer = God

I flew up to San Francisco to meet with the producer John Montoya. He was working on a new TV series called 'I Love Flipper.' My agent said he was considering me for a lead role.

I met up with John at a private party being held at Caffe Proust. When I walked in, John was talking with his brother, Baby Jim. John was wearing a full-length fur coat; two small dogs were barking at the bottom of his coat. John ignored the dogs and hurried over to give me a hug. "Hey Man..."

"John..."

He gave me a look. "Listen, you can't call me 'John.'"

"Oh. Sorry baby."

"In this town they call me '2 Cold.'"

"Right, right. '2 Cold.' Got it."

He nodded. "It's just too cold for me here. I can't roll with it. L.A.'s my town."

"I hear that."

2 Cold pointed to his brother. "This is my bro, Baby Jim."

We shook hands. "Good to meet you."

"You too."

2 Cold put his arm on my shoulder. "Come on. I'll get you a drink."

He began steering me toward the bar. The dogs trailed after 2 Cold's fur coat. I saw Anne Heche talking to Emilio Estevez.

We stepped up to the bar. I noticed that Miss P herself was bartending. I smiled my tough-guy-with-love smile and looked into her eyes. "How are you, baby?"

Miss P grinned. "Fine, thanks. What can I get you?"

"A Bud, please."

2 Cold looked at Miss P. "Make that two Buds."

"Sure."

2 Cold turned to me. "Let me tell you about the show."

"Yeah, baby. Lay it on me."

"I want to do a show that's totally retro, you know?"

"Right on."

"And I want to take the best stuff from the best shows."

"Talk it like you walk it."

"Exactly."

Miss P reached across the bar and handed us two bottles of Bud. I smiled at her. "Thanks." I left a $5 bill on the bar.

2 Cold took a sip of his beer. "What I want to do is take part of 'I Love Lucy' and mix it with 'Flipper.'"

I gulped my beer. "Yeah, baby."

"And maybe a little bit of 'Leave It To Beaver.'"

"Absolutely."

2 Cold adjusted his coat. Several gold chains jingled around his neck. He looked at me. "So I need to get the good-looking Ricky Ricardo guy who teaches the dolphin, you know? 'Cause it's all about their relationship. Each week we gotta learn more about them, you know?"

I nodded. "Yup. That's it."

Suddenly, Baby Jim walked up to 2 Cold. "Your lady's getting hit on by Anne Heche."

2 Cold looked at Baby Jim. "Anne Heche is digging Warmer Parts."

"That's what I said."

2 Cold looked around the room for a moment. Then he turned back to Baby Jim. "Cool."

Baby Jim nodded. "Just thought you'd want to know." He took a sip of his drink and walked away.

2 Cold adjusted his fur coat. He took a sip of his beer and stared out across the room. "Yeah, all my ladies, man…But Warmer Parts, you know…She and I are tight, you know?"

"Yup."

"Rick James has his Mary Jane. I got my Warmer Parts."

"Right on."

He took a sip of his beer. I finished mine and motioned to Miss P for another.

2 Cold looked at me. "Are you and Roseanne still kickin' it?"

I shook my head. "No. That ended years ago."

"Oh…" 2 Cold stared off across the room. He took another sip of his beer. Then he turned to me. "Anyway, I'm gonna make this show a big hit. And I'm gonna need that Ricky Ricardo, dark-haired, handsome dude, you know?"

"Sounds great."

"I mean, you hear me, right?"

"Yeah."

I nodded. Miss P handed me another beer. "Thanks."

I turned back to 2 Cold. He took a sip of his beer. "And I'm gonna need you, too."

"Huh?"

2 Cold nodded. "Yeah. I need someone to play Big Craig. He feeds flipper. Each week he falls into the tank and they have to pull him out. He makes a big splash, gets all water-logged. They have to pull him out before he drowns. The audience'll love it."

"Oh…"

"You'll be perfect. How much do you weigh?"

I put down my beer. "I...I'm not sure."

"You gotta find out, man. Have your agent call me. We'll get some clothes fitted for you, okay?"

"Uhh...sure..."

"Okay, great...Listen, I'm gonna go talk to my lady. But you enjoy the party, okay?"

"Right."

2 Cold spun around in his fur coat and walked off across the room. For a moment I watched the two little dogs jumping at the bottom of his coat. Then I picked up my beer and took a gulp.

A Bird in the Hand

On Thursday afternoon, I swam for about 40 minutes at the Loudon Club pool, then did a UVA tan session. I did a quick set of weights after the tanning session, then showered and put on a black T-shirt. I stepped out onto Sunset and felt the warm sun on my arms and face. I was looking good.

At the next intersection, a young, dark-haired actress walked up to me. She was wearing mirror sunglasses. I recognized her. Chickie Vaughn, the woman who'd screen-tested for the Dave Mathews film that got canceled by Miramax. Chickie pushed her sunglasses up into her hair and smiled. "Excuse me, do you know where the nearest ATM is?"

I grinned at her. "I sure do."

"Great. Where?"

I paused. "Do you have a pen and paper?"

"Oh, you don't have to write it down. You can just tell me where it is."

I winked at her. "Actually, I was gonna write down my phone number?"

"Why?"

"Don't you want my phone number?"

Chickie looked at me. "Well, I want to know where I can find an ATM."

"You don't have to be shy. You're really asking for my number, right?"

"No, I really just want to know where I can find a cash machine."

"Really?"

"Yes."

"Are you sure?"

"Yup."

"Oh."

She put her sunglasses back on. "So is there an ATM around here?"

"I think there's one near the In-And-Out-Burger." I pointed toward the next corner.

Chickie looked where I was pointing. "Okay, thanks." She walked away.

The Sisters of Mercy

I was at a party at The House of Blues in honor of the Olsen Twins, Mary-Kate and Ashley. Forbes Magazine had just rated the twins' combined assets as the 20th largest economy in the world. The sisters had rented out the House of Blues to celebrate.

Whoopi had arranged for me to go as her guest. She put my name on the guest list. When I arrived, I drifted around looking for her. I couldn't find her. Eventually I gave up and found my way to the bar.

I stepped up the bar. I tried to flag down the bartender, but accidentally bumped into Candace Bergen. I grinned at her. "Hi, baby. How are you?"

Candace looked away. "Uhh, fine."

I smiled again. "Good."

The bartender came over. I nodded at him. "A vodka seven for me, and the lady will have a…"

"A Calistoga, please."

I looked at her. "Nothing to drink, baby?"

She turned to the bartender. "Just a Calistoga, thanks."

The bartender disappeared. I turned back to Candace. "Last time I saw you was so awesome, baby."

"Really? I left you in handcuffs. I just split."

I nodded. "Don't I know it. I've never been so turned on in my life. Nothing compares to that. Even when Barbra was tying me to her bed one time, and she had these leather spikes on, I wasn't—"

"Please—" Candace put up her hand to stop me. "I don't want to hear about it."

"Okay."

The bartender came back with our drinks. "One vodka seven…and… one Calistoga." He set the drinks in front of us.

I handed him a $20 bill. The bartender shook his head. "There's no charge, sir. It's a free bar."

Candace explained, "The Olsen's are paying for it."

"Oh, cool." I turned to the bartender and handed him the $20. "Well, take this for yourself then."

He waved the $20 away nervously. He glanced up and down the bar. "I'm sorry, sir. No gratuities are allowed. The Olsen's are making sure we get paid."

"Oh...okay"

The bartender hurried away. I turned to Candace. "I'll have to go find the sisters and thank them."

She took a sip of her Calistoga. "Fat chance of that."

"Why?"

"You wouldn't get near them. Even Regis couldn't get back there."

"What do you mean?"

"Look." Candace pointed to a private room off to the side of the lounge. Several large men in tuxedos stood in front of the door. I recognized one of them from my gym. "That's where the twins are hanging out. They've only allowed Ashton Kutcher and Keanu Reeves back there so far. Just watch."

I took a sip of my drink. I could see David Schwimmer step up to the door. He said something to the guy from my gym. The guy looked at him for a moment, then shook his head. Schwimmer said something else. Another man stepped in front of him and shook his head emphatically. Schwimmer's face sunk. He turned and began to walk slowly away.

I turned to Candace. "Wow. That's harsh."

Just at that moment, Jennifer Aniston walked up to the men. They nodded at her and opened the door. Jennifer stepped quickly inside. For a split second, I thought I caught sight of one of the twins sharing a glass of champagne with Bill Gates. But then the door closed.

The bartender noticed us looking at the room and stepped behind us. "Can I get either of you another drink?"

Candace gestured with her Calistoga. "No, thanks. We still have these."

"All right."

I took another sip of my drink. "But baby, I'm almost ready for another."

She shook her head. "Go easy for once. You always drink too much."

I nodded. "All right."

I took another sip of my drink and turned back to watching the Olsen's private room. One of the men was turning Courteney Cox away. Courteney walked off glumly. I gestured at the room. "I wonder what their parents think of all this…"

Candace was sipping her Calistoga. "What's that?"

I gestured toward the Olsen's room again. Sandra Bullock was being ushered quickly into the room. "The twins. What do their parents think about this kind of thing?"

Candace looked at me for a moment. She paused. "You mean you don't know?"

I looked at her. The bartender seemed to be listening too. I leaned in close. "Know what?"

Candace lowered her voice. "Well…no one really knows where their parents are."

"Really?"

"Yes…" She leaned close. "Their parents disappeared right after the girls turned twelve. No one's seen them since."

I shook my head. "Naw, that can't be. I mean, who takes care of them?"

Candace glanced nervously at the bartender, who was hovering behind us, drying a beer mug. She looked at me. "Maybe we shouldn't talk about this now."

"No, it's okay. I don't mind."

She looked at the bartender for a moment. "No, I mean it. Not now."

"But baby…"

She finished her Calistoga, set it on the bar, and walked off. I watched her walk away then ordered another drink.

Boat Drinks

I was at the producer 2 Cold Montoya's wedding reception. It was being held on a cruise ship anchored in Marina del Rey. I stepped up to the bar to order a drink. Sinbad and David Hasselhoff were leaning against the bar, ordering shots of tequila. When I finally caught the bartender's attention, I ordered a quick vodka-seven.

As the bartender started pouring my drink, Sinbad turned to me. He looked at me for a moment. "Wassup, man?"

I nodded. "Hey."

The bartender handed me a drink. I put a $5 bill in his tip jar. Sinbad squinted at me. "Aren't you that guy who was in those toilet commercials?"

I grinned and took a sip of my drink. "Yup. That was me."

Sinbad laughed. "Shoot, man. That was so wack. Buncha guys attacking a giant toilet bowl. Me and my buddies used to laugh our asses off whenever that came on."

I took another sip of my drink. "Thanks."

Hasselhoff threw back his tequila. "I remember that." He clapped Sinbad on the back. "That was crazy."

"Yeah."

I started to say "Thanks," but Sinbad had already turned back to his drink. I gestured with my glass to Hasselhoff and set off across the deck.

I strolled casually along the promenade, wandering toward the back of the boat. Suddenly, I bumped into Barbara Walters and Cher. They were laughing and talking. Barbara was wearing a pink dress. Cher was wearing dark pants and a dark blouse, partly unbuttoned. Her cheeks seemed unusually shiny and rigid—as if they were being pulled taut across her cheekbones. I took a sip of my drink and tapped Cher on the shoulder.

"Baby, can I just say that I love your Malibu house. It looks awesome."

Cher smiled. "Thmph-yun."

I paused. "What's that, baby?"

"Thmph-yun."

Barbara looked at me. "She said, 'Thank you.'"

I nodded. "Oh, right."

Cher nodded. "Umph-lub-in-too."

I looked at Barbara. "What was that?"

"She said that she loves it too."

"Oh...good."

We stood around for a moment. I took a sip of my drink. Barbara pointed at Cher. "She just came back from Dr. Herbert."

"Oh."

Cher touched my arm. "Wheh-din-yah-say-mah-has?"

I grinned. "What's that?"

"Wheh-din-yah-say-mah-has?"

I squinted at her. "Huh?"

"Teb-meh, wheh-din-yah-say-mah-has?"

Barbara smiled at me. "She wants to know when you saw her house."

I shook my head. "I don't know. Fairly recently. But listen, I should probably get going. I wouldn't want to interrupt you lovely ladies. You were busy talking and all..."

Barbara grabbed my arm. "No, no. Stay a while. Tell us something about yourself."

"Umm, well...I can't." I downed the rest of my drink and looked at them apologetically. "I'd love to stay and chat, but I have to get a refill."

Cher nodded. "Ah-kay."

Barbara smiled politely. "Well, it was wonderful to see you."

"You too."

I hurried back to the bar.

The Big Cheese

A few minutes later, I spotted 2 Cold standing by the front of the boat. He was sipping a glass of bubbly champagne. I strolled up to him. He saw me and reached to give me a hug. "Hey, man…"

"Hey, baby."

I swept a hand around the boat. "Great party."

2 Cold nodded. He smiled happily. "I've got two more of these planned."

"What's that?"

2 Cold took a sip of his champagne. "I'm working with a producer from MTV-Japan. We're gonna do three weddings and pick the best footage from all three. I want to run it as a kind of 'Real World' in Hollywood."

I paused. "That's brilliant."

2 Cold took another sip of champagne. "Best part is that I'm not even getting married."

"Wow."

I took a sip of my drink. 2 Cold clapped me on the shoulder. "Come on, I want you to meet someone."

I followed him across the boat. After a minute, we stepped in front of two identical looking men in suits. 2 Cold introduced me.

"Fellas, this is the guy I was telling you about."

"Hey."

"Hey."

We all shook hands. 2 Cold put his arm around my shoulders. With his other hand, he pointed at the two guys. "Ed and Jon are gonna do a new version of 'The Munsters.' It's gonna be animated."

I took a slug of my drink. "Uh-huh."

"But here's the best part. It's gonna be spelled 'M-u-e-n-s-t-e-r-s,' like the cheese."

"Oh…cool."

"Yeah, and all the Muensters are gonna be made out of cheese."

"Wow."

2 Cold indicated me to Ed and Jon. "This is the guy who should do the voice for the owl."

Ed looked at me. "Let me hear you say something like 'Who's there?' But put the accent on the 'Who.'"

I nodded. "Okay." I paused and took a deep breath. "Who's there?"

Ed and John looked at me for a moment. Then they started laughing. They slapped each other on the back. "He's perfect. Wow, man. He's so great. I can't believe it."

2 Cold smiled. "Didn't I tell you?"

Ed handed me his business card. "Call me on Monday."

I took the card and looked at it for a moment. "Yeah. Okay."

2 Cold took another sip of his champagne. "Listen, I better check on the film crew. I'll see you in a bit, okay? Just make yourself at home."

"Sure thing."

2 Cold downed the rest of his champagne. "I'll call you when I know when the next wedding is."

"Okay."

"Thanks."

2 Cold walked off. I knocked down the rest of my drink and went back to the bar.

I'll Give You a Tip

I had just eaten a good steak dinner at the Sea Palm Grill in Venice. I was walking out to my car when the restaurant's manager came running after me. He tapped me on the shoulder. "Ahh...sir...if you have a minute..."

I stopped and turned around. "Sure, baby. What's up?"

"Well, it's, ahh...I was wondering...did you, uhh...did you find the service here to be adequate?"

I smiled. "Oh, absolutely. Karen was a sweetheart. Kept checking to see if I wanted another beer or anything. Just terrific."

"And the food was okay?"

"Yeah. I loved it. Just like my mom used to make."

The manager shifted his feet. "Well, I was wondering then, ahh...I noticed that you didn't leave any sort of gratuity, or anything...for Karen..."

"Yes, I did."

The manager paused. "Well, there was a piece of napkin on the table..."

He showed me the napkin. I nodded. "Yup. That's it."

The manager took a pair of reading glasses out of his shirt pocket. He looked at the napkin. "...It has some numbers written on it. I'm not quite sure what that is..."

I nodded again. "Yeah. That's my phone number."

The manager looked up at me. His reading glasses were perched on the edge of his nose. "I don't understand."

"I figured I'd give Karen my phone number. This way she can call me."

"For what?"

I smiled. "Well, there was just this vibe, you know...I could just tell that she dug me."

The manager looked at me. "Karen's married."

"Oh."

"To me."

I patted the manager on the shoulder. "Oh, well...cool. Then you know what I mean."

The manager shook his head. "I'm not sure that I do."

I nodded. "Well, that's okay." I reached into my pocket and pulled out a $10 bill. I handed it to him. "Here you go. Make sure Karen gets this." I turned and walked out to my Hyundai.

Tech Boom Splat

I was at Natalie Merchant's house in Los Feliz. She was throwing a big vegetarian bash to celebrate her new album 'Intercontinental Holistic Missile.' I made sure to fuel up on a big steak before the party.

When I got to Natalie's place, I ran into Shannon Doherty at the bar. I ordered a glass of wine and gave Shannon my tough-guy-with-a-heart smile. "Hi, baby."

"Hi, yourself."

Shannon turned to the bartender. "Un vodka con hielo, por favor." She turned back to me. "You're looking good."

"So are you."

The bartender poured Shannon a drink. She thanked him and put a $20 bill in his tip jar. I suddenly realized that I'd forgotten to tip the bartender. I quickly stuffed a $5 bill in his jar.

I picked up my wine and followed Shannon toward the living room. "So what's new with you?"

Shannon was balancing her vodka carefully. The bartender had filled her glass to the brim. "Umm...just some auditions...What about you?"

"Same."

Shannon stopped and took a sip of her vodka. Then she smiled at me. "Mmm…Yum."

"Yeah, baby."

Suddenly Chickie Vaughn burst into the room. "Hey everybody. Come quick. Moby's on the roof. He says he's gonna jump."

"OH MY GOD."

A herd of people suddenly rushed out to the backyard. I found myself being swept along by the crowd. I saw the producer Vin Blunno race past me. David Schwimmer bumped into me. Some of my wine spilled on David's shirtsleeve; he didn't seem to notice.

We hurried out to the backyard and looked up at Moby. He was barefoot and wearing jeans, but no shirt. I could see his toes poking over the edge of the patio roof, just above my head. I heard Sally Field say to Vin Blunno, "Does anyone know where Natalie is?…Maybe we should get her?"

Everyone was looking up at Moby. He seemed greatly upset. David Schwimmer called up to him. "Come on down, Moby. Please come down. We love you."

Several other people nodded. "Yeah, we love you. Come on down."

Moby looked down at us and screamed. "NO…Nobody understands me. I can't stand it anymore."

I looked up at Moby. "But, Moby, you're the voice of rock 'n roll. We need you—"

Moby gestured angrily with his hand. "I hate rock 'n roll. I hate it. I don't want any part of it." Saliva dribbled out of his mouth. He wiped his lips with the back of his hand. "See. No one understands me."

I tried again. "But baby—"

Suddenly Shannon Doherty grabbed me by the collar. She yanked me backward. "Hey, you're not helping."

I turned to her quickly. "I'm sorry, baby. Moby needs me."

I turned back to Moby. He was pointing down at us. "I'm gonna do it. I'm gonna jump."

William Shatner was standing directly under Moby. He turned to the crowd and waved his arms. "For God's sake, give him room. Give him room."

Moby wiped more saliva from his chin. "I can't stand it anymore. I'm gonna jump. I'm gonna jump."

Suddenly he made a piercing shriek and lifted his arms. He began flapping them and jumped off the roof.

He landed next to William Shatner. Almost instantly he screamed. "My foot. My foot. Oh my God. My foot."

Shatner looked at him. "What's wrong, man? What's wrong?"

Moby pointed to his right foot. "My toe. My toe." He screamed again.

Shatner put his hand to his forehead. "My God."

The crowd watched for a moment longer, then began to drift away. I heard Sally Field mutter, "I could use a martini."

I looked over at Shannon Doherty. She'd finished her vodka. I gave her my full-muscle smile, the one where I clench up my neck to show off my upper body tone. "Want another drink?"

"Sure thing."

We walked back into the house and headed for the bar.

Vodka Weather

I was at a party at Georgia's, talking to Faith Hill. She was glowing with happiness. "Joe Guerriero is just the greatest," she said. "I'm so in love."

I patted her on the arm. "That's great, baby."

"He's so kind and considerate. So loving, so—I mean, he's just really something."

"He's something all right."

"Yeah."

Faith smiled at me. "Listen, I need to go to the ladies room. Can you wait for me? I'll be right back."

"Sure thing, baby. I'm just gonna get a drink."

"Okay."

Faith walked off. I stepped up to the bar. The bartender squinted at me. "What can I get you?"

"Another vodka seven, please."

Suddenly Faith Hill rushed back to me. She grabbed my arm. "DAMN IT."

I spun around. "What, baby? What did I do?"

She gestured toward the back of the room. "I was walking to the bathroom and I spotted them." She pointed toward Joe Guerriero and shook her head. "That bastard."

I glanced over at Joe. He was standing in the back corner, talking closely with Chickie Vaughn.

I turned back to Faith. "What, baby?"

Her face darkened. "He's hitting on her."

"No, he's not."

"Yes, he is."

I looked over at Joe and Chickie again. "How can you tell?"

Faith glowered. "He put away his cell phone."

"Ohhh..."

Faith's eyes started to grow wet. Her voice choked up. "That bastard..."

The bartender handed me my drink. I thanked him and put my arm on Faith's shoulder. "Come on. I'll buy you a drink."

Faith nodded. "Yeah. Good idea." She turned to the bartender. "A double vodka, please."

The bartender started pouring her a drink. I rubbed her shoulder gently and took a sip of my drink.

S.P.E.C.T.R.E.

I was sitting at a booth in the NoHo diner with Sandra Bullock, Chickie Vaughn, and the cartoonist Scoops Nolan. We were eating hamburgers and fries. Sandra ordered a vanilla coke. We were having a great time. Scoops had just told the joke about Ted Danson acting his way out of a paper bag. We all laughed hysterically. Chickie laughed so hard that tears came to her eyes.

Sandra took a sip of her vanilla coke. "You guys are the best. I am having so much fun."

"Cool."

I was still chuckling over Scoops' joke. I looked at Sandra and smiled. "Hey, Sandy, I gotta ask you something."

Sandra took another sip of her vanilla coke. "What?"

"Well, it's pretty wacky and you'd probably, uhh—never mind."

"No, what?"

"Well, we're having such a great time and you seem like such a nice person. I don't want to offend you or anything…"

Chickie poked me in the arm. "Just ask her. You can't start a question like that and then not ask."

Sandra nodded. She slurped down the last of her vanilla coke. "Yeah—what were you gonna ask?"

"Well, you gotta promise not to get mad."

Chickie looked at me. "She can't promise that."

Sandra smiled. "Yeah, just go ahead and ask."

I paused. "Well, all right. It's just—it's the damnedest thing. I've heard this wacky rumor a couple of times, and I know it's just something that someone must have made up somewhere—"

Sandra's face darkened. "What kind of rumor?"

"Well, it's so stupid."

"What is it?"

I shook my head. "It's so silly. It's just something ridiculous. Like, you belong to a super-secret organization that controls Hollywood. That's how you got your start in movies or something. You and Keanu. I mean, it's so obviously false—"

Sandra stared at me. "Who told you that?"

"I don't know. I mean, it's just something I've heard, here and there… But it's so ridiculous, right?…"

Sandra pulled a pad and pen out of her purse. She looked at me. "Tell me their names."

"What names?"

"Anyone you spoke to."

"I don't know. I don't really remember."

She squinted at me. "Who-was-it?"

I swallowed nervously. I could feel Chickie and Scoops watching me. "Well, uhh…maybe there was this make-up woman at Paramount… uhh, I think her name was Missy—but that's all I remember. I swear."

"Are you sure?"

"I promise."

"All right. I believe you." Sandra scribbled something in her notepad then put it back in her purse. She looked at us. "What a silly rumor. Of course it's not true." She looked around the table. "Who wants dessert?"

None of us answered.

Sandra looked at us. "Come on—who wants dessert? I'll buy."

After a moment, Chickie said, "Umm...I could eat some rice pudding...if someone'll split it with me."

Sandra looked at me. "You'll split that rice pudding with Chickie, won't you?"

I swallowed. "Oh, absolutely. Absolutely. I love rice pudding."

Sandra motioned to the waiter. The rest of us sat in silence.

Cool Nights, City Lights

Later that night, Chickie Vaughn, Sandra Bullock, and I were walking out to our cars. Scoops Nolan had left earlier in the evening. Chickie suddenly pointed up at the night sky.

"Look at all those stars."

I looked up. "Yeah, baby."

Chickie waved her hand. "Wow. I think I saw a shooting star."

"Cool."

Sandra and I helped Chickie into her Camaro. I gave Chickie a quick kiss on the cheek. "Okay, baby."

Chickie smiled. "See, you're not such a bad guy."

"You know it."

"I'll call you soon. We'll do lunch."

"How about sushi?"

She started her car. "Naw, I hate sushi."

I nodded. "Okay. Whatever you want, baby."

"All right."

She drove off.

I said a quick good night to Sandra Bullock and walked over to my car. I found my keys and climbed in. Then I turned the ignition and switched on my headlights.

I shifted into first gear, and was about to drive off when suddenly I noticed Sandra standing directly in front of my car. My headlights burned a bright yellow against her tan legs. She was staring at me.

I poked my head out the window. "Is everything okay, baby?"

Sandra continued to stare at me.

I shifted back to neutral, pulled the brake, and hopped out of the car. I ran over to her. "Baby, you startled me. I almost drove right into you."

Sandra looked at me. "Are you a team player?"

"What's that?"

"Are you gonna play ball?"

I looked down at the ground nervously. "I love to play ball. Any kind of ball. My dad thought I should've been a quarterback. But then I was a lifeg—"

"You know what I'm talking about."

"I don't, baby."

Sandra pointed a finger at me. "I can make life very good for you, or very bad. What's it gonna be?"

I swallowed nervously. I tried to give her my big-guy-with-a-soft-inside smile. I could feel my heart pounding in my chest. "Oh, baby, I know I've made some mistakes. But I want to be good. Trust me."

Sandra raised her hand and poked me sharply in the chest. "Then start keeping your big mouth shut."

"It's shut, baby. Absolutely shut."

Sandra grinned. "Good. Just play ball and you'll be fine. You hear me?"

"Sure thing."

Sandra nodded. "Okay, great. I'm glad we had this talk." She patted me on the shoulder. "Have a great night." She turned and walked away.

I turned and climbed slowly into my Hyundai. I reached for the stick shift but my hand was shaking uncontrollably. I waited a few minutes, then finally drove home.

Funeral for a Friend

I was standing on line at the bank when I ran into Candace Bergen. She was wearing sunglasses and flipping through the latest issue of 'Variety.' I walked up behind her and whispered in her ear. "Hi baby."

Candace spun around. "HUH?"

I smiled at her. "How've you been?"

She lowered her sunglasses. "Oh...it's you."

"It's me."

She smiled. "What's going on?"

"I just did the Heston funeral."

"Really? You went to that?"

"Yup."

"How was it?"

"Great. I rocked it."

"What do you mean?"

"Best gig I had in a while."

"It was a funeral."

The person ahead of Candace stepped up to the next teller. We moved forward in the line. I nodded. "Yeah, I know. But I had a speaking part."

"A speaking part?"

"Yeah, Lenny asked me to give a short speech. And I nailed it. I had all my lines down and everything. It just flowed. Whoopi said I did a great job. I think it might lead to some other work."

"Uh-huh."

One of the bank teller's said, "Next." Candace turned to me. "See ya." She stepped up to the teller. I continued to wait in line.

Celine on Me

I was at Caesar's Palace, trying to get backstage to see my old roommate, Celine Dion. I had always tried to keep in touch with her from the days when we were both just starting out in L.A. Reporters from PEOPLE Magazine and Entertainment Magazine were milling around in front of Celine's dressing room, waiting to catch a word from her. A security guard was checking for my name on the guest list. He looked up and down the list. "Sorry sir. I don't see your name on here."

I smiled. "That's okay. You can just tell her I'm here."

"Sorry. I can't do that."

Just then, Celine's dressing room door swung open. Celine leaned out. "Gary, can you do me a favor?"

The two magazine reporters tried to jostle for position. The security guard turned to her. "Yes, ma'am?"

"Can you get us some lemons and some chamomile tea?"

"Sure thing."

I waved at Celine. "Baby, how are you?"

Celine stared at me. "Oh…hi…"

I stepped over to her doorway. "Baby, I didn't hear from you. I thought I'd come down and see how you're doing."

One of the reporters took out a mini cassette recorder. Celine glanced at the reporter quickly then looked at me. "I'm kind of busy."

"Don't I know it. You're playing Vegas. Me doing auditions. We've got it going ON."

Celine touched my shoulder. "I have to run."

I smiled. "Oh…okay. I just wanted to tell you not to be upset about doing Vegas or anything. Just enjoy it."

Celine squinted at me. "I am enjoying it."

"Wow, really? Remember how you used to say that Vegas is where people go to die?"

The reporters leaned in. Celine shook her head. "I never said that."

"Yes you did."

"No I didn't."

"Sure you did. When we were sitting at Denny's that time…remember? The night you decided to try that laser eyebrow thing."

"Shhh…"

"No, it was when you got your ears done. I think that was it—"

"SHHH."

"—Or that crazy nose doctor with the German accent. I always mix them up. Those were great times, remember?"

Celine glared at me. "SHHH."

"What, baby?"

"I have to go." She ducked into her room and shut the door.

I looked at one of the reporters. "She didn't used to be like that."

The security guard started to push me away. I turned and walked back to the casino.

Ovitz and Out

Ovitz and I were sitting in the bar at the Hotel Roosevelt, talking about women, baseball, and life. Mel Gibson was supposed to join us. But he called from his car to say that he couldn't make it. Ovitz was hurt that Mel was blowing him off. He threw back his martini. "Jesus. Mel doesn't have time for me. My ex-wife wants more alimony. I can't get arrested in this town."

I took a sip of my whiskey. "Come on, Mike, you're the king. You and Geffen, man. You guys are it."

He shook his head. "I don't feel like I'm 'It.'" He waved to the bartender for another martini.

We sat quietly for a moment. The bartender shook up a new martini and set it down in front of Ovitz.

I gestured to the bartender. "Put it on my tab."

Ovitz looked at me slowly. "You don't have to do that."

I patted him on the back. "It's no problem, baby."

Suddenly Christina Aguilera drifted through the lobby with her entourage. I waved at her. "Christina, baby, I love you...come have a drink with me and Mike Ovitz."

Christina strolled over to us. Two of her bodyguards followed. Christina's hair was braided with little red-white-and-blue ribbons. Just as she stepped in front of us, I caught sight of a shiny silver ring piercing her navel. She smiled at us politely. "I'm sorry, do I know you?"

I raised my whiskey. "Baby, we bumped into each other at the post-party, you know, after the Heston funeral thing."

Christina looked at us. "I wasn't at the Heston party."

I looked at her. "Oh, baby, I'm sorry. I had you confused with someone else. Can you forgive me?"

"It's all right."

She started to walk away, but I pointed at Ovitz. "Hey, Chrissie, you know Mike Ovitz, right?"

She paused. "Umm...I know the name..."

I nodded. "Everybody's heard of him. He's the best agent in Hollywood."

Ovitz stood up and shook Christina's hand. "Pleasure to meet you."

Christina turned to her bodyguards. "You guys can go get a drink or something." She waved them away and they drifted off. Christina took a seat next to Ovitz.

Ovitz lifted his martini. "Here's to you, Christina. You and I could make millions together."

"I've already got an agent."

"Oh, really. Who?"

"Brad Grey."

"Oh...I'll get you away from him eventually."

I tapped Christina on the shoulder. "Baby, do you want a drink?"

She smiled. "Are you buying?"

"I sure am."

"Okay. A whiskey sour."

I turned to the bartender. "One whiskey sour for this fine lady, please."

The bartender hurried off to make the drink. I turned to Christina. "Baby, you are so fine."

Ovitz slugged his martini. "Damn right. She's finer than frog's fur."

Christina giggled. "I've never heard that one before."

"What? 'Finer than frog's fur?'"

"Yeah."

The bartender brought over Christina's drink. I nodded at him. "Put it on my tab, Darryl."

The bartender squinted at me. "It's David."

"Oh, right." I handed the drink to Christina. We all clinked our glasses and sipped our drinks. I looked at Christina and smiled. "Baby, you are finer than the finest grain of sand."

Ovitz nodded. "You are finer than the finest Persian silk."

Christina giggled. She pointed at me and said, "I like it better when he tells me how fine I am."

I patted her arm. "That's right, baby. I know just how fine you are."

Ovitz took another sip of his drink. He looked at Christina intently. "Well, let me tell you, words can't begin to express how fine you truly are."

I nodded. "Yeah. Scientists can't even measure a grain of sand as fine as you."

Christina laughed. She touched my arm. "You are so funny."

Ovitz glared at me. "Yeah, he's funny all right."

I looked at Ovitz. "Come on, Mike, lighten up."

Christina nodded. "Yeah, lighten up, Mike."

Ovitz frowned. "I'm trying to talk business here and you're getting in the way."

"I'm not getting in the way."

"Yes you are."

I turned to Christina. "Baby, if Mike and I keep arguing like this, we're gonna end up going "No I'm not,' 'Yes, you are' until both of us throw up our hands and say, 'FINE.' But let me tell you, you are finer than both those 'Fines' put together."

Christina touched my leg. "WOW. You are so funny."

I grinned. "Baby, you are finer than all the fines I've ever paid for overdue library books."

Christina giggled out loud. Her breasts started to tremble with laughter. "Ah-hah-hah..."

Ovitz slugged down his drink and stood up. "That's it. I'm out of here."

I waved casually at Ovitz. "Okay, Mike, see ya."

Christina continued touching my leg.

BEEP

It was a Tuesday evening. I was drinking a six-pack or two of beer and talking on the phone with Joe Guerriero. Suddenly my call waiting beeped.

"Hey, Joe, I got a beep. Can you hold?"

"Yeah."

I clicked the 'Flash' button on my phone. "Hello?"

"This is Jeff Berg at ICM. Let me speak to Steve."

"That's me."

"Real quick, Steve, I'm just calling to—"

"Hey, can you hold one sec?"

"No, I—"

I clicked back to Joe. "Hey, it's some guy, Jeff Burns at IMT, or something? Who is that?"

"JEFF BERG?"

"Yeah, that's it."

"HE'S THE PRESIDENT OF ICM."

"Really?"

"YEAH. YOU HUNG UP ON HIM?"

"No, I just clicked back to you."

"TAKE THE CALL."

"Really?"

"YES."

"Okay, I'll call you back."

"Bye."

I clicked back. "Hey, Jeff, sorry man. I was on with my buddy, Joe Guerriero. We were talking about some commercials that—"

"Listen, Steve, real quick, I can't have you for the Heston tribute. We're going to go with Oliver Platt. Sorry. Good luck."

"Actually, Jeff, that's fine. I thought Oliver was terrific—"

"Okay. Gotta run."

"Listen, while I have you on the phone, I thought I'd mention that I'm—" Just then my call waiting beeped. "—Oh, hang on a sec, Jeff."

I flashed my phone. "Hello?"

"Hi, baby."

"Whoopi?"

"Yeah."

"Baby, listen, I'm on with Jeff Lerner at IMT."

"I don't know him. I know Jeff Berg at ICM."

"Yeah, that's it. I gotta take the call."

"All right. Let me know if you get the Heston thing."

"No, I didn't."

"Oh, child, I'm sorry."

"No, it's cool. Something else'll come up."

"All right. Love'ya."

"Love'ya."

I clicked back to Jeff. "Sorry about that. It was Whoopi. She always asks me if—"

"STEVE?"

"Yes?"

"GOODBYE."

Jeff hung up. I waited a moment, then dialed Joe back.

It's All about Who You Know

A month later, something amazing happened. It was 9 am I was still sleeping. The phone rang. I answered it dreamily.

It was my agent calling. He said that David Mamet was producing an updated version of 'Capricorn One' and Jonathan Demme was slated to direct. Demme had been talking to one of the producers of 'Speed 3.' The producer had mentioned the Demme project to Sandra Bullock and she'd personally recommended me for a part in 'Capricorn One.' Sandra said I was exactly what Demme needed.

My agent laughed loudly into the phone. "Apparently, it took Demme two weeks to find out who you were."

"Damn."

"Anyway, he wants you to play the part that O.J. Simpson played in the original."

"What's that?"

"You'd be one of the astronauts. You're supposed to go to Mars, but NASA fakes the whole mission."

"Wow."

"Yeah. You gotta go over and meet with Demme at 3:00."

"Cool. That's great."

"Yeah."

I paused. "Is it a big part?"

"Well...you'll have some lines. But O.J. didn't say much in the movie, so I'm not sure. But they've already signed Julianne Moore, I think. So it's gonna be pretty big."

"This is so great."

"Call me when you finish."

"I will."

"Okay."

"Bye."

We hung up.

At 3 pm I drove over to Demme's studio on Lot C. When I walked in, they were screen testing Josh Brolin for some kind of part. I spotted Julianne Moore talking with someone in a side office. A secretary led me into a lounge. After a few minutes, Demme came into the room and shook my hand. "All right, let's do this."

Demme walked me into a small studio. I noticed a blue screen against one wall. Demme pointed to the floor near the blue screen. "I want you to get down on the floor over there. When I say action, I want you to pretend you're in pain. You'll say, 'There's no water, there's no water.' Think you can do that?"

"Yup."

"And when you say it, picture yourself stuck in the middle of a desert. You're tired. You're hungry, you're dying of thirst. Okay?"

"Like when I'm out of beer?"

"Huh?"

"I'll pretend it's like when I'm out of beer."

"Ohh...well, if that works for you."

I nodded. "Believe me, when the cooler's empty, I'm scared."

"Okay, sure. Let's do that."

"Okay."

Demme stepped back. I walked over and kneeled down on my hands and knees. Demme tapped the cameraman. "Okay...places...marker..." I looked down at the ground. Suddenly Demme yelled, "Action."

I stared hard at the ground for a moment. I contorted my face in a grimace of pain. I tried to picture all the times when I'd run out of beer. Suddenly I pounded my fist into the ground and said, "There's no water...THERE'S NO WATER." Then I stared hard at the ground.

After a moment, Demme yelled, "Cut."

I stood up and walked over to him. "How was that?"

He smiled. "Looked great to me."

"Cool."

Demme huddled with one of his assistants. "Just give me a second. I want to play it against the blue screen." He disappeared into a control room.

I waited for a moment. For some reason I felt strangely calm. I looked at the cameraman and nodded. He waved back.

Suddenly Demme came back into the room. "I like it. I like it a lot."

"YEAH?"

"You look great. I want you in this picture."

"Wow, really?"

He nodded. "Yup."

"That's great."

We shook hands. Demme patted me on the shoulder. "I'll call your agent. I'll get back with you in the next few days. We'll have you meet

Julianne and everybody. I think we'll have Billy Paxton on board by then, too."

"Great."

"Well, terrific. I'll see you in a few days."

"Thanks."

"My pleasure."

I walked out to the parking lot and climbed into my car.

I couldn't believe my good fortune. My first feature. I was finally on my way. I put the key in the ignition and gave it a good turn.

I revved my Hyundai's proud engine a few times. Then I drove off into the sunset.

THE END